Wild
Food

Biddy White Lennon is a journalist, specialising in Irish food culture. She has published twelve books, eight about Irish food history, ingredients and recipes, including *Best of Irish Festive Cooking, Best of Irish Home Baking, Best of Irish Traditional Cooking, Best of Irish Potato Recipes, Best of Irish Meat Recipes, Irish Cooking*.

As an actress since early childhood Biddy appeared in films, TV, theatre, and in the long-running RTÉ drama 'The Riordans'. Starting with radio and TV drama, writing gradually took over from acting. Biddy is a founder member, former chairwoman of the Irish Food Writers Guild, a committed member of The International Slow Food movement and active member of The Slow Food Sugarloaf Convivium that in 2012 organised the enormously successful Wild & Slow Fest, the first-ever food festival entirely devoted to wild food.

Evan Doyle opened his first restaurant in Clifden, County Galway, in 1985, and followed this with the original Strawberry Tree Restaurant in Killarney, County Kerry, in 1988. In 1999, together with his two brothers, Evan opened The BrookLodge Hotel in Macreddin Village, County Wicklow and it is here that today's Strawberry Tree restaurant showcases artisan and locally produced organic foods. In 2004 The Strawberry Tree became the first and only certified organic restaurant in Ireland.

Evan is a member of Eurotoques and has hosted the National Food Forum and the very first Wild Food Festival. He is involved in the Slow Food movement and is a founding member of The South Dublin/ Wicklow Convivium. Evan is Chairperson of The Taste Council of Ireland and is a Director of The Organic Trust.

Wild
Food

ature's Harvest: How to Gather, Cook & Preserve

Biddy White Lennon   Evan Doyle

THE O'BRIEN PRESS
DUBLIN

First published 2013 by
The O'Brien Press Ltd.,
12 Terenure Road East, Rathgar, Dublin 6, Ireland.
Tel: +353 1 4923333; Fax: +353 1 4922777
E-mail: books@obrien.ie
Website: www.obrien.ie

ISBN: 978-1-84717-467-3

A catalogue record for this title is available from The British Library.

1 2 3 4 5 6 7 8 9 10
13 14 15 16 17 18 19

Front cover photograph courtesy of iStock
Typesetting, editing, layout and design: The O'Brien Press Ltd
Printed and bound in the Czech Republic by Finidr Ltd.
The paper in this book is produced using pulp from managed forests.

To our fellow foragers

ACKNOWLEDGEMENTS

Thank you to Áine Ní Mhaoldomhnaigh-Ó Drisceoil for assistance with the botanical names in the Irish language.

PICTURE CREDITS

WARNING

Contents

A Lifelong Passion

I have been foraging for wild food for as long as I can remember. The concept of the wayside nibble on the way home from school was then still a normal part of a rural child's day. Strictly speaking, I wasn't a rural child. I'm a Dub – born, bred and brought up in Dublin between three houses.

There was my father's which had a tiny, paved and completely barren roof garden, my mother's which boasted a balcony overlooking a now-lost Dublin green space in Upper Ely Place where there were brambles and a few apple trees, and my grandparents' in Merrion Square where residents paid an annual subscription for a key to the square which was then a rather wild place with just a few trees that provided food – hazel, sweet chestnut, elderberries and wild strawberries. There was also a keeper who considered these treasures to be perks of the job.

The real opportunity to forage came when we decamped, from June to September, to live in our seaside summer shack in Danny's field in Donabate, north County Dublin. My earliest (and almost only) memory of my father was going out early onto the links golf course, which backed onto the field, to gather mushrooms for breakfast. He played a few holes of golf and I looked for field and St George's mushrooms.

We explored hedgerows for berries, caught crabs and gathered mussels and clams when the tide was out, sometimes swopping them for sea bass, plaice, or dabs from people fishing from the rocks.

A lifelong friend describes my brother and myself as feral. Both parents worked and only made fleeting visits. Sometimes they brought delicious cheese, ham, smoked fish and packets of pasta from Smith's or Findlater's and left money for us to buy food. But bread and milk aside we preferred to spend it on ice-cream and ginger beer and to forage for food.

As I grew up need turned to love. I found books, the most influential of which was *Wild and Free* by Cyril and Kit O'Ceirin. The idea of preserving wild food had never occurred to me. Denis, my husband, and Dairsie, our son, became enthusiastic preservers. We walked miles, exploring different habitats in woods, fields and sea shores, in search of the makings of jams, chutneys, wild wines and beers. Our house had the aromas of a brewery and a jam factory combined.

To me wild is still wonderful. It gives a point to a walk to come home with something tasty to eat, to preserve and give as gifts. As a committed and active member of Slow Food I was entranced by the idea of working with my friends in the Sugarloaf Slow Food Convivium to organise the first ever Wild Food Festival in Europe. I learned a lot during the year of preparation. The Wild & Slow Fest in November 2011 was an enormous success. Join with us in the immensely enjoyable, healthy activity of harvesting the abundance of wild foods.

Biddy White Lennon

The Long Field, The Strawberry Tree and The Food Story at Macreddin Village

· ·

We have all grown up with The Long-Field. City folk see it as green ditches with no footpaths as soon as they have escaped the Urban. Cattle and sheep view it as manna from heaven when they escape out on to it from their closures and rural folk, well rural folk are always delighted to inform their fellow farmers that it is their stock that has escaped onto The Long-Field and not their own.

Cattle and sheep love The Long-Field; they know that The Long-Field is brim-full with goodies. Unfortunately, for them, forward planning has never been a talent common to either sheep or cattle, and come sunrise the glorious rebels are inevitably spotted ambling aimlessly along the nearby country roads, out on The Long Field, and are duly rounded up.

The Long Field is the 327,258km of common Irish grass verges and hedgerows. Our lush damp climate produces a stunning array of wild foods, from fresh spring herbs to summer berries to autumn mushrooms and nuts.

I first came across The Long-Field when, still as a teenager, I found myself managing a restaurant in Galway. It was there that

The Strawberry Tree wild garlic harvest.

I met with the ever-eccentric Gerard M King from Connemara. Gerard imparted, during foraging walks, his extensive, infectious knowledge on the culinary uses of wild herbs, wild greens, wild mushrooms and indeed wild berries that still affects the menu in The Strawberry Tree to this day. These were foods with 'A Story', today we might call it Provenance … but it affected my view of foods forever.

In quick succession, I opened two restaurants. However, it was The Strawberry Tree that fully encapsulated this ethos. On the opening menu, I wrote boldly across the top: Sea Foods, Farm Foods and Wild Foods - not in any glib or flippant manner, but simply because the story of the Quay, the Field and the Wild had become important to me.

That was twenty-five years ago and my very first menu paid homage to the 'Story behind the Food'. The menu named the fabulous producers of the foods for the restaurant, and I wrote about the wild foods that accompanied these treats. The Strawberry Tree

The Strawberry Tree, Wild Food Pantry.

had nailed its colours firmly to the flag pole.

In 2002 The Strawberry Tree became the only Irish restaurant to achieve EU Organic Licence status. Food with traceability, sustainability, zero tolerance of chemicals, good animal husbandry and naturally grown are the foundation of this licence. Under EU legislation, my kitchens are audited annually by both the Department of Agriculture and by The Organic Trust.

However, my love of wild foods and their provenance is equally as strong. The Strawberry Tree successfully achieved EU Derogation to continue to serve wild foods on its Organic Licensed menu.

Since 1988, we have set out daily from The Strawberry Tree kitchens to harvest wild foods either to present on the night or to save in the traditional manner by preserving with sugar or drying or pressing or oil or alcohol. The traditional manner is of the most importance to us; wild foods preserved in jars, demi-johns or Kilners have a much more visual worth and become much more precious than wild foods simply put in a freezer.

The wild food pantry is just for the chefs of The Strawberry

Tree. In an 'all-fresh kitchen', it's an extra gift to them. In November to be able to un-bottle something like the 'summer sunshine of the May elderflower' is truly stunning.

Some years ago, I moved the wild food pantry from the kitchen into the restaurant, simply to show our guests how precious these foods are to us, how we gather them, and how we use them on our menu.

Wild foods are now highly fashionable. When I advertised for a full-time forager recently, the media were straight on to me looking for the story. There was no interest two decades ago when I first sought a wild food forager for The Strawberry Tree!

Slow Food addressed this newfound public desire for wild food education by hosting the world's first Wild Food Festival here in Macreddin Village. Nigh on 3,000 people attended and 1,100 sought knowledge on wild foods through over twenty workshops. I was honoured that Macreddin Village was chosen as the host location.

My chefs still escape onto The Long-Field, daily, to harvest wild foods for The Strawberry Tree menu. The sight of chefs in 'whites', totally focused on what is growing wild in the hedgerows, lifts my heart … as I hope it does those of our guests as they drive up to the Village.

Here are some of our wild food recipes: some 'old with tradition', 'some new with a twist'. Enjoy!

Evan Doyle

The Strawberry Tree wild cep harvest.

How the Book Works

This combined field guide and cookbook, inspired by the growing interest in wild food, is an introduction to harvesting nature's bounty.

It follows the gradual emergence from dormancy of wild plants. Beginning in Feburary, with the wild nettle, when you can harvest its tender shoots, over ten months it explores two dozen other wild food plants, finishing with the wild sloe in November, the close of the wild food gathering season.

The wild food calendar shows at a glance when each wild food is likely to be ripe for picking and the length of time over which it is harvested.

However, a particularly early spring, or a late, cold, sunless spring, or a mild and dry autumn, or harsh winter frosts, arriving before we have had time to enjoy autumn, cause a certain amount of variation. Aspect and altitude play a role. South and west-facing plants bloom and fruit earlier than those facing east or north. Plants growing close to sea level come early and the higher the altitude the later the harvest.

We have selected but a few of the thousands of possibilities, choosing those we felt were the most prolific, widely available geographically, versatile and particularly good to eat. We have included just four easily identifiable fungi. Mushroom-hunting is specialised and, even though there are lots of books on the thousands of varieties of wild mushrooms, if our selection whets your appetite, our best advice is to go to one of the many tutored mushroom-gathering field walks led by experts.

Similarly, if you develop an interest in fermenting and brewing, there are clubs for enthusiasts where you can learn the finer points of making country wines and beers.

Each section is designed to enable you to learn how to identify each wild food, the habitat in which it thrives, where to look, what it looks like, when to look, how to harvest, how to prepare it for eating, and traditional uses and methods of preserving the wild food.

Then come the recipes. Some that Biddy White Lennon has developed over many years of home cooking and food writing that reflect the way families eat today. Renowned wild food cook Evan Doyle provides others. Evan is well known for his creative use of wild food and his recipes that feature on the menu at The

Strawberry Tree, his fine-dining restaurant at The BrookLodge Hotel, Macreddin Village, near Aughrim, County Wicklow.

Evan and his team preserve wild foods in a variety of traditional ways that are used for the menu in the Strawberry Tree Restaurant in Macreddin Village. His recipes also include enticing ways of preserving wild foods. Throughout this section there are many recipes for turning fresh wild foods into wonderful preserves that can be enjoyed throughout the winter and can be given as gifts to friends of all ages. Such a gift can go far beyond the pleasure of eating the food; it can open minds to the bounty of the land which is available year after year and free for the picking.

PRESERVATION

. . . .

This section explains the principles of preserving food, using traditional low-tech methods of preserving sweet and savoury preserves, chutneys, pickles and drinks. Methods of making these preserved foods can be applied to many of the featured wild foods. In order to avoid repetition you will be referred to this section.

Finally, we offer advice on sustainable, responsible wild food gathering and ways of protecting the wild food plants for the generations to come to enjoy.

You will be surprised, once you start looking, how quickly the eye learns to recognise edible plants. No matter what season, open the book and check out what wild food you might come across on a walk. Giving a point to a walk doubles the pleasure, and cooking and eating triples it.

A Charter for the Sustainable Harvesting of Wild Food

- Foragers should respect the plants, the environment as a whole, and take into consideration the need to share some wild plants with the wildlife of the area and take account of the rights of landowners.

- Foragers should also respect other foragers; although no wild foods belong to any of us, we should all respect each others 'patches'.

- Unlike cultivated foods that are planted by humans for a single quantifiable harvest, wild foods are an occurrence of nature and a full understanding and appreciation of this haphazard propagation when it comes to harvesting should never be underestimated.

- While Ireland has abundant wild food plants, and only a very few of our indigenous and naturalised wild plants are on the 'at risk' list, foragers should guard carefully what we have so that the generations to come can enjoy our wild food.

- It's crucial to learn how to harvest without destroying a plant, a tree, a mushroom, seashore vegetable, or seaweed.

- Wild plants regenerate themselves naturally, either

by spreading their seed or spores, by re-growth, or by creeping rhizomes, or self-rooting arched branches.

• Cutting hedgerows before the berries are harvested is wasting food, depriving both birds and humans.

WILD HERBS AND GREENS

By their nature wild herbs and greens have very loose roots. Great care must be taken when harvesting leaves not to disturb the root mass, eg pull up or move a wild sorrel plant and that's the end of that plant. Harvest the larger leaves and allow the small ones to grow on and you can harvest it all summer and in years to come.

WILD FLOWERS AND BLOSSOMS

Although wild flowers such as the primrose are more than pleasing in summer salads, the centre of all wild flowers is the seed for the next generation and needs cross-pollination by bees and insects to give us next year's wild crop. Blossoms are flowers that give us fruit, eg apple blossom and rose blossom. If you pick these beautiful flowers for your salads, you get no apples or rosehips. It is best practice to pick wilting blossoms, after cross-pollination, and pick just the petals not the fruit centre.

WILD SEAWEEDS

Seaweed can only regenerate if it is cut leaving several inches on the plant which will, in a year or eighteen months, grow again. If you harvest seaweed by pulling it from the rocks with the 'holdfast' attached, it dies. Seaweeds and sea plants have a season that is later than land plants, maybe by two months. Do not harvest too early; give the weeds and plants a chance to propagate.

WILD FRUITS

We won't get the fruits unless we have left the blossoms. The elder tree is a prime example for the forager. Pick all the flowers in spring for your elderflower wine and then you don't have elderberries for your game dishes in the autumn. Meantime, you've also deprived the bees of their harvest and cross-pollination of the flowers, and also deprived the birds of a feast and, by default, the natural dispersion of next year's seedlings.

WILD MUSHROOMS

Fungi grow from spores in the ground. Pick an elderly wild mushroom that is past eating and you have prevented the spores needed to grow fungi in that place next year. Many 'new foragers' seem to have got into the habit of bringing back large 'trophy' mushrooms to show-off. These are usually mushrooms that are not firm and are well past their eat-by date. Mushrooms like these should be left to spore for next year's crop and it is not good sustainable practice to pick them.

BEST PRACTICE

DO leave at least a third of the blossom, flowers, berries, seed heads, nuts, leaves, seashore vegetables and seaweeds on the plant and cut, don't pull.

DON'T break branches to make gathering easier.

DON'T pick or bring home fungi that is over mature.

DON'T venture onto private land without permission.

DON'T pick plants in conservation areas where there is a Department of the Environment, Heritage and Local Government notice that states you should not do so.

DO take care where you park your car.

DON'T block farm gates.

DO close all farm gates after you.

DO bring all your litter home.

DON'T dig up wild plants.

Forager's Calendar

Wild Nettle	February–August
Dillisk	February–November
Carrageen	February–November
Wild Garlic	Early March–May
Wild Sea Beet	March–November
Wild Rock Samphire	March–November
Wild St George's Mushroom	April–August
Wild Sorrel	April–November
Wild Hawthorn	May–November
Wild Elderflower	May–Late June
Wild Sea Lettuce	May–November
Wild Herbs and Flowers	May–September
Wild Strawberry	June–Late September
Wild Chanterelle	July–November
Wild Bilberry	Late July–August
Wild Field Mushroom	Late July–October
Wild Blackberry	August–October
Wild Rowanberry	August–Late October
Wild Damson	August–September
Wild Cep, Penny Bun	August–November
Wild Crab Apple	September–Late October
Wild Elderberry	Early September–October
Wild Hazelnut	September–November
Wild Rose	September–November
Wild Sloe	Late October–Early December

Preserving Wild Foods

Traditional methods of preserving food include drying, salting, fermenting, pickling in oil, in alcohol, with sugar or honey, lactic fermentation, smoking and excluding air.

HOW PRESERVING WORKS

The action of enzymes, yeasts, moulds and bacteria result in all food deteriorating unless action is taken to destroy, halt or slow down the process. The action of enzymes, for example, can be halted by heating food to boiling point (100°C) for a short period and by simple preservative chemicals like salt and acid solutions like vinegar. The action of yeasts and moulds can be slowed by drying. However, their action can cause useful fermentation (as in wine and beer making). Unwanted bacteria can be controlled by drying, pickling and cooking.

SALT turns water in food to a strong solution of salt and when combined with drying makes this even stronger and through a process of osmosis prevents bacteria and micro-organisms.

SUGAR does not stop enzyme action but most foods preserved by sugar are also cooked or fermented.

PICKLING is a preserving medium with a strong salt or acid content. Immersing food in vinegar or brine or a mixture of both is a traditional preserving method. Highly acidic solutions and strong salt solutions prevent micro-organisms from growing and enzymes from working. The term pickling includes a strong vinegar solution, and also the salt curing of meat and seafood. Vinegar supplies the acid to many pickles and often the addition of sugar and salt provides an extra safeguard. Some foods are prepared in brine only and fermented by naturally present bacteria which produce lactic acid (for example Sauerkraut). Pickling also covers the mixture of salt, saltpetre and spices used to cure meats like bacon and salt (corned) beef. Mustard seeds, ground or whole, also help preserve the food and are a common addition. Vinegar used for pickling should be 6% acid.

SMOKING is almost always used in combination with other preservation methods such as drying or salting, or (in hot smoking) cooking. Smoking dries the outside of foods and seals the surface with an airtight, antiseptic surface.

OIL-immersed foods will keep indefinitely. Traditionally,

such foods are either briefly blanched in water, or water and vinegar, or salted, as an additional safeguard.

ALCOHOL is a most effective preservative. The higher the proof (%) the better it works. Liquids that are less strong often have sugar added as bonus preservative.

DRYING is a method used for many foods, eg mushrooms, berries, flowers, seaweeds, vegetables, herbs and fruit. Drying removes most of the moisture, inactivating the growth of micro-organisms (although it does not kill them). Bacterial cells are destroyed as water evaporates and the concentration of salt and sugar increases.

Practical Methods

• •

DRYING

• •

There are a number of different methods of drying: either outdoors in sunshine and (preferably) low humidity, or indoors in a sunny room like a conservatory.

AIR-DRIED Outdoors during a dry spell (again preferably when humidity is low); or indoors in an airy place – a roomy clothes dryer is worth experimenting with.

OVEN-DRIED In a conventional oven set at a very low temperature (you may need to leave the door ajar to achieve the correct temperature); or in a dehydrator. The ideal drying temperature is 30–34°C. After the first few days the temperature can be reduced to 25–26°C. When ready, leaves are brittle and flowers should rustle but not crumble. Dried foods need cool, airy, dark, dry storage conditions.

Drying blossoms and flowers

Gather on a dry day after any morning dew has dried off and the flowers have just bloomed. Flowers wilt quite fast so work quickly.

First shake them gently to get rid of insects. If they look very dusty, rinse quickly with cold water. Spread them out on a rack fitted with a fine mesh, or a basket, so that they do not touch each other. The air must be allowed to circulate freely. Outdoors choose a dry day in a shaded, sheltered place so that they don't blow away. Indoors you can speed things up by fixing a fine mesh frame above a radiator. Stir them occasionally and allow a few days at least. Before storing, remove the stems and leaves and any green parts. Flowers keep their colour best if light is excluded. Choose a cardboard box, or a tin with a tightly-fitting lid, or wrap glass jars with brown paper.

Drying leaves

Leaves are dried in a similar way to flowers, or hung up in bunches before stripping from the stem and storing.

Drying mushrooms

Cut off the base and wipe with a damp cloth. If the mushrooms are large they should be cut into slices. Thread onto a thin twig or use a darning needle and very thin string, or very thick button thread; a knot between each piece keeps them separated and allows them to dry faster. Hang the twig or thread in a dry, warm place. Once they are fully dry they may be stored in jars or paper bags; storage must be in a dry, dark place.

Drying berries

Berries are best spread out on a baking sheet and oven-dried. The most suitable varieties are those with a robust skin like elderberries and sloes.

Drying seaweeds

Traditionally air-dried out of doors in sunny breezy weather; they can also be oven dried. Crumble before storing.

PRESERVING WITH SUGAR

Sugar is the active preservative of wine, beer, jam, jelly, syrup cordial, bottled fruit, flavoured spirits, chutney, pickles and similar sweet/sour preserves. The amount needed varies due to the presence of natural sugars in many foods.

Fruit is often bottled in sugar syrup. Water and sugar are cooked together until the sugar is dissolved. 1 litre water/½kg sugar gives a medium, sweet syrup while 1 litre water/1kg sugar gives a heavy sweet syrup.

Bottling Fruit and Berries

The strength and whether you choose a light or heavy syrup depends on the type of fruit and on how sweet you prefer the finished result. Place the water and sugar in a pot and heat gently until the sugar is dissolved. Boil for a minute or two. Use sterilised jars with glass or metal lids.

Pack tightly into the jar, filling them a third at a time and adding the sugar syrup to the level of the fruit as you go. It will take about 125ml of syrup to each 500ml fruit.

Place jars on a rack or a tea towel in the bottom of a pot, choosing a large pot deep enough for the water to cover the jars by 3cm. Pour hot water over. Bring to the boil for approximately 15 minutes.

Remove from the pot and place on a wooden board or a tea towel to cool. Wait 24 hours and then test the seal. The lids of screw tops should have pulled down into a slightly concave position as they cool. This indicates a good seal. If it pops up when you press the top, you do not have a good seal. To test the seal on glass jars with rubber seals and a clamp on top, press the fruit against the lid. If any bubbles appear, you do not have a good seal. It is possible to reprocess at once. Otherwise, eat the food as soon as possible as it will not keep. Correctly done and stored in a cool dark place, they will keep for a year.

Making Fruit, Berry, Blossom or Hip Cordials, Syrups and Dessert Sauce

• •

Place prepared fruit in a pot and cover with water. You need ¼ litre of water for every 1kg fruit. Simmer until soft and the juice extracted. Some berries like rowan and blackberries may need to be mashed to release the maximum juice. Strain the mixture through a jelly bag allowing it to drip overnight. Do not squeeze the bag.

Measure the juice and calculate the amount of sugar needed. The amount varies according to the tartness of the fruit and how sweet and concentrated you want the finish product to be. Typically you'll need about 300g sugar for a litre of juice.

The sugar is added to the juice, heated gently until fully dissolved, and then boiled for up to fifteen minutes, or until it has reached the desired consistency. Ultra light for cordials, light for syrups, and heavy for concentrated dessert sauces. Skim any scum from the top before bottling in small sterilised bottles with tightly-fitting corks or caps. Once opened, syrup needs to be used within a week and is best stored in the fridge. If you see any signs of mould on the surface, it is wise to play safe and dispose of the remainder. If you desire extended storage, follow the method for sterilising bottled fruit.

Making a Berry or Blossom Liqueur

1 bottle of your chosen spirit which should be at least 40% proof

Sufficient prepared berries or blossom to half-fill a bottle (in the case of blossom it is best to use just a 700ml wide-necked jar)

Sugar to half fill, or to taste

Using a funnel, fill the bottle or jar about one third full of sugar. In order to extract juice, hard-skinned berries (like sloes) must first be pierced with a sharp fork or darning needle before placing at once into the bottle or jar. To dissolve the sugar and release the juice, shake once a day for seven days, then once a week for seven weeks.

Some are ready for use after a few months; others are better left for a few more months before straining and decanting the liquid alone into a fresh bottle. The remaining berries may be processed through a food mill and the boozy pulp used to add flavour to desserts, cakes and ice cream.

Making Jam, Jelly, Fruit Butter and Fruit Cheese

• •

Success depends on the interaction between sugar, pectin and acid. The proportion of sugar to prepared fruit is usually 1 to 1. Some fruits are recognised as low in acid and/or low in pectin, and need additional acid or pectin to get good results. When needed, recipes will include apples or liquid pectin and often lemon juice. The method common to all is to weigh the prepared fruit, then simmer in a large wide pot with a little water until soft. Remove the pot from the heat and stir in the warmed sugar; then place over a gentle heat and stir until sugar is dissolved. Now boil rapidly for about ten minutes, or until setting point is reached (105°C). Take off the heat and skim using a heated metal spoon. Cool a little before pouring into warm, sterilised jars. Fill to the top to exclude air and cover.

The final cooking process for fruit butter and fruit cheese is different to jam and jelly where the mixture is boiled rapidly until the mixture reaches 105°C. Fruit butters and cheeses are brought briefly to boiling point and then the heat is reduced and the mixture simmered, stirring frequently, until the mixture is thick and a wooden spoon drawn across the bottom of the pan leaves an area clear of the pulp. The pulp has reached the correct consistency for fruit butter when the area clear of the pulp is narrow. To reach the thicker consistency of a fruit cheese it is necessary to continue simmering until the area clear of the plup is wider.

SALT/BRINE

If you want to be successful preserving food with salt, do not skimp on the time required or amount used. Keep to the instructions. For example, if it states a certain concentration, or rubbing in salt for a certain number of days, follow the recipe.

A typical solution would be 2–3 15ml tablespoons of salt to each litre of water.

VINEGAR/ACID

The concentration matters. A good rule of thumb is never use a solution containing less vinegar than water. Some foods are preserved in all vinegar, some with added water or other acids, like lemon juice, and some with added sugar.

OIL

Oil will preserve food, but you must ensure the food is completely covered in oil and air excluded. The recipe may say that certain foods need to be blanched first, don't be tempted to skip the process or you won't get a good result.

SMOKING

Fish and meat are amongst the most common foods smoked.

Fish smoking is an ancient method of preservation in all northern countries. Wood smoke contains tarry substances which when deposited on the food contribute to preservation by killing bacteria. Smoking dries the surface of the food, sealing it from air, and adds flavour. A contemporary spin is the smoking of mushrooms and shellfish.

Wild Nettle

* *

Urtica dioica * Irish *neantóg*

Wild nettle is a perennial herb – a weed in the wrong place, a versatile and tasty food in the right place. From the eighteenth-century proverb comes the expression 'grasping the nettle'.

> *Tender-handed stroke a nettle*
> *And it stings you for your pains;*
> *Grasp it like a man of mettle*
> *And it soft as silk remains*

Nettles, having been eaten, enjoyed and used as a spring tonic in Ireland since ancient times, fell from favour in the nineteenth century. In the 1840s a series of famines struck when potato blight destroyed the potato crop, the staple food of ordinary people. Wild leaves such as nettle, charlock and wild garlic were relied on for nourishment to keep people alive. Afterwards, nettles and similar wild leaves came to be associated with poverty and starvation.

WHERE TO LOOK

* *

Naturally a woodland plant, nettles grow pretty well anywhere, are rich in natural chemicals that improve the circulation, provide relief from age-old ailments like rheumatism, lower high blood

pressure and high blood sugars, and purify the digestive system. Tender young leaves were traditionally eaten as a spring tonic. The Scots liked them so much they used to grow them under glass as an early kale.

WHAT IT LOOKS LIKE

Nettles can grow over a metre tall; the leaves are covered with stinging hairs. When it emerges from the ground the leaves are soft and pale green, the stem tender. As it matures, the leaves darken, the stem thickens and dull flowers appear in between each group of leaves.

HOW TO PICK

If you don't want to put your faith in grasping the nettle, wear gloves. Only the tender young, pale green leaves are good to eat. Older leaves have a coarse texture and a bitter taste. If you identify a convenient patch, cut the stems to ground level regularly and the creeping root system will produce young leaves from early spring to autumn.

HOW TO PREPARE

Strip the leaves from the stem. A quick rinse in cold water and they are ready for use.

TRADITIONAL USES

To kill off the formic acid (contained in the sting) nettles must be cooked. Nettles are used much as you would spinach, spring cabbage, or kale, and recipes are interchangeable. Butter and nutmeg were often used as a flavouring. The traditional Irish and Scottish soup – *brotchá* (a broth) combines barley or oats, onions, milk, butter and nettles and wild garlic. It was also served in the form of a thick gruel, or porridge. After potatoes arrived nettles were often substituted for grains, and nettle champ became popular. In Northern Ireland chicken was boiled with chopped nettles, wild garlic, leeks, and oatmeal to make a popular dish. Nettle was once added as a flavouring to Scottish haggis and Irish white puddings. Nettle beer has a lovely, distinctive flavour and, with a little mint, is a light and thirst-quenching drink. A contemporary spin flavours the beer with root ginger and lemons.

PRESERVING WILD NETTLES

Nettles can be brewed and fermented into beer and wine and used to make a herbal tea. The leaves may be dried using the method outlined in the Preservation section.

Typical quantities brewing nettles into beer

Use equal quantities by volume of nettles and water, ½ of sugar, 25g cream of tartare, and one lemon; 10g of fresh root ginger, 2g dried hops (optional), and 4½ litres water.

Typical quantities for fermenting nettles into wine

The amounts for wine are a 2-litre container packed fairly closely with nettle leaves to 1½kg sugar, 10g root ginger and two lemons, white wine yeast, and 4½ litres of water.

WILD NETTLE AND POTATO SOUP

WHAT GOES IN

100g wild nettle leaves, picked carefully!

10g wild garlic leaves

350g old organic potatoes, roughly chopped

1 large organic onion sliced

1 stick of organic celery, chopped roughly

1 organic leek, sliced

2 bay leaves

1 litre organic vegetable stock

50ml organic cream

Organic olive oil, sea salt, black pepper and ground nutmeg

A little wild garlic pesto or cream and a little nutmeg

HOW IT GOES

In a large pot, heat oil and simmer onions, celery and bay leaves together until soft. Add the leeks and cook for a few minutes, season lightly with the sea salt, black pepper and the ground nutmeg, and then add in the potatoes. Stir everything together and pour in the vegetable stock.

Bring to the boil, then simmer until the potatoes are soft.

When potatoes are cooked, add in the wild nettles and wild garlic, cook for a few minutes, remove from the heat and blitz in a processor until smooth.

Wild Nettle and Potato Soup.

HOW TO FINISH

Pour soup purée back into the pot; add cream to a pleasing consistency, reheat and season with sea salt and black pepper as desired. Serve with a swirl of wild garlic pesto or cream topped with ground nutmeg.

WHAT YOU GET

Is a perfect transition from the heavy winter-warmer style soups to the lighter style of summer! Flavoured with the last of the winter leeks, thickened with fabulous floury old spuds and combined with the first taste of spring with the baby wild nettles and the hint of wild garlic, this is a perfect early spring soup.

WILD NETTLE BEER

5 litres of water

Wild young nettle leaves, enough to fill a 5-litre bowl by volume

500g sugar

10g root ginger

30g cream of tartare

1 lemon, rind and juice

30g beer yeast

30g dried hops (optional)

Place sugar and cream of tartare in a lidded fermentation vessel.

In a very large pot boil the nettle leaves, ginger, lemon rind and hops (if using) for 10–15 minutes.

Strain the liquid through a sieve into the vessel. Stir and allow cool to room temperature. Stir in the lemon juice and sprinkle the yeast on top. Cover with a cotton or muslin cloth and allow ferment for four days. Carefully skim the surface to remove any scum or froth. Using a siphon, rack the liquid into bottles with a swing action beer lid or, if you prefer, into a demi-john and cap with a rubber bung.

Store for a week in a very cool place. Then it is ready to drink. Take care when you open the bottles as, depending on the success of the fermentation, it may be very fizzy indeed.

WILD NETTLE TEA

Fresh or dried leaves can be used to make a traditional spring tonic herbal drink. The leaves should be infused for at least ten minutes.

3–5 young nettle tops
200ml boiling water
Honey or sugar to taste

As it tastes better hot rather than cold a simple method of keeping it hot while it brews is to place the nettle tops in a vacuum flask or vacuum cup. Pour on the boiling water. 10 minutes later (or whenever suits you) pour through a strainer into a mug and add honey or sugar to taste.

Wild Dillisk (Dulse)

Palmaria palmata * Irish *duileasc* and *creathnach*

Dillisk (In Irish the larger and smaller types are *duileasc* and *creathnach*; the latter refers to the smaller plant which grows on mussel shells. In Northern Ireland it is called dulse in English) is popular for its unique rich, salty, nutty taste. It can be eaten raw, fresh, or dried. It has been used as an ingredient in cooking and as a savoury nibble by children and adults for hundreds of years.

WHERE TO LOOK

Found on the low to middle shore. It may grow from clumps from the edge of rocks, in rock pools underneath other seaweeds such as kelp or wrack. In subtidal areas it may even grow from these large seaweeds. The smaller types can grow on mussel shells.

WHAT IT LOOKS LIKE

Dillisk may be reddish-brown, or a very dark red colour; the feel is tough and leathery. The holdfast is disc-shaped and the flat fronds grow directly from the holdfast. The shape of the fronds may vary from a fan-shape to single leaf and although often fairly short they can, in favourable conditions, grow quite long.

HOW TO PICK

You can pick right through from spring to early autumn. Time your gathering to arrive as the tide goes out. Every two weeks there is a 'spring tide' which is the best time to harvest seaweeds. At this time, the tide goes out further than usual. A spring tide has nothing to do with springtime but refers to a springing of the water. The tides with the largest range are usually in February/March and September/October. Usually two days either side of a full or a new moon are the best time. For clambering over sharp rocks it is best to wear non-slip, tightly-fitting swim-shoes to avoid cuts. Wellingtons are not a good idea. Perhaps take a change of clothes in case your enthusiasm to gather results in getting wet!

Most seaweeds should be harvested by cutting with a sharp knife or scissors. On no account should you pull so hard that the holdfast comes off the rock or the host seaweed. Do not over-pick.

HOW TO PREPARE

Give a rinse in fresh water to wash off the sand – a hose works well. Pick off any bits of shell or other seaweeds.

TRADITIONAL USES

· ·

At the Old Lammas Fair in Ballycastle, Northern Ireland (held continuously since 1606), there have always been (and still are) stalls selling dillisk or dulse. Dillisk is more usually eaten fresh and raw when it is similar to chewing gum (but with more and longer lasting flavour, a savoury nibble to keep hunger at bay). Also eaten crisped in the oven, or even fried in butter until crisp and placed between two slices of bread.

Widely used to add flavour to potato dishes like a dillisk champ, it is frequently added to soups, stews, salads, bread, oatcakes, biscuits, and in a coating for fried or baked fish (in addition to oatmeal, or in place of breadcrumbs).

PRESERVING SEAWEED

· ·

Drying

This is the traditional method of preservation.

Spread on the grass for several days to allow sun and rain to dry and bleach. In dry weather you see a layer of dried salt on the fronds. When dry and crisp it is ready. Store in a cardboard box or in brown paper bag in a cool dark place. It will keep for a year or more.

Salted

Grind or crumble the dried seaweed and mix with sea salt and store in a dry place. Use in a salt grinder or mill.

WILD DILLISK AND
LEMON CREAM

WHAT GOES IN

50g wild dillisk, dried

1 organic onion

1 stick of organic celery

1 organic bay leaf

250ml organic white wine

400ml fish stock or organic vegetable stock

250ml organic cream

2 lemons, juiced and zested

Organic olive oil, sea salt and black pepper

HOW IT GOES

Cook the onions, celery and bay leaves together in a little oil until soft. Add white wine and reduce to one quarter. Pour in fish stock and cream, and reduce to a sauce consistency. Add in dillisk and lemon zest. Simmer for 3 to 4 minutes. Remove from the heat and blitz in a processor or with a hand blender.

HOW TO FINISH

Strain through a sieve and pour back into the cooking pot. Season to taste with salt, pepper and lemon juice.

WHAT YOU GET

Is a fab taste of the ocean and the perfect accompaniment sauce for any white fish. As clean in your mouth as an oyster from the

Weir, or as fresh as a deep breath of Atlantic sea-spray on the west coast. Use with flat or round fish and impress all at dinner.

FRESH MACKEREL OR HERRING WITH A DILLISK AND OATMEAL CRUST

A TRADITIONAL DISH

4–8 fresh mackerel or herring fillets, depending on size

8 tbsp (heaped) of oat flakes

15–30g dried dillisk

2 eggs beaten

A little white flour

Butter

Remove stray bones. Wash and dry fish. Mix oat flakes and dillisk.

Set up a production line and first dip fish into flour, then beaten egg, then the oat flakes and dillisk mixture. Allow to rest in a cool place to let coating set. Melt butter in a large pan; when just beginning to foam add the fish and cook on one side until the coating is browned, turn, and brown the other side. You may need to cook in batches but this is best served hot and crisp from the pan.

DILLISK OATCAKES

The Irish and the Scots love their oatcakes – a savoury biscuit not a cake. The name derives from a Scandinavian word *Kaak* or *Kake*, meaning any flat bread. As the climate of Scotland and much of Ireland suited oats more than wheat, even biscuits were often traditionally made from oatmeal.

225g medium ground oatmeal
30g plain white flour
About 75ml boiling water
60g butter, melted
1 large pinch bicarbonate of soda
A large pinch of salt
3 level tbsp dried dillisk, crumbled into very small pieces

In a bowl mix the flour and oatmeal together. Pour the boiling water into a cup, add the butter, salt and bicarbonate of soda and mix this into the oatmeal and flour. Mix quickly and knead into a ball. It should be firm but not dry. Depending on the absorbency of the flour and oatmeal, you may need a little more. Sprinkle flour on a working surface and roll out the dough into a flat circle about 18–23cm in diameter. If it splits, just press it together; it is very forgiving. Slide on to a baking sheet and trim the edges neatly. Cut into 8 triangles or farls. Bake at 180°C for 45 minutes. When done it should be lightly tinged with brown. Store in an airtight tin.

Wild Carrageen

Chondrus crispus & *Mastocarpus stellatus* * Irish *carraigín*

Carrageen is a catch-all term for two types of seaweed: *Chondrus crispus* and *Mastocarpus stellatus*. Both of these were traditionally harvested as carrageen and used for the same purpose. In Irish food culture the most widely known is carrageen jelly or carrageen blancmange. However, carrageen also features as a thickening agent and flavouring in seafood, fish soups, sauces, ice-cream, jam and jelly. Many of us eat it every day in commercial processed foods such as ice-cream, dressings, sauces and jams. Even in the English language carrageen goes by various names: it is also known as Irish moss or carrageen moss.

WHERE TO LOOK

Both types are found on the mid to lower seashore, on poorly drained rock surfaces and rock pools. Look when the tide is going out, particularly at spring tide and a few days either side of a full and new moon.

WHAT IT LOOKS LIKE

This small plant has a flattened stem which divides and subdivides into a fan shape. In suitable growing conditions it grows in

Carrageen tends to grow underneath other seaweeds like these.

thick masses of a purplish-red, reddish-brown, or reddish-green colour. Between 7–15cm long, the fronds are attached by a round holdfast which should *not* be pulled off or the plant will not regenerate. It can look quite different, depending on the conditions in which it is growing. In sheltered estuaries the stalks may be short and the fronds bushy with lots of divisions; while in wave-exposed shores the stalk is longer, the plant narrower and the branching sparser.

HOW TO PICK

As it is often quite short it is best to cut with a scissors, taking care not to pull off the holdfast.

HOW TO PREPARE

Rinse in fresh water to wash off the sand – a hose works well. Pick off any bits of shell or other seaweeds.

TRADITIONAL USES

Carrageen belongs to a group of seaweeds that are used as a source of *agar*, a Malayan word meaning a gelatinous extract made from these plants. As well as thickening and setting liquids it is used in toothpaste, medicines and cosmetics and for clarifying beer.

Unlike other seaweeds, carrageen is not eaten raw but cooked in liquid until it has more or less dissolved and is then strained through a fine sieve to remove any remaining visible carrageen.

Carrageen was dissolved in milk (or something stronger) as a treatment for coughs and chest complaints. Being high in iodine and a storehouse of vitamins and trace elements, it was supposed to be good for healing burns, getting rid of worms (in humans and animals) and indigestion.

PRESERVING CARRAGEEN

Drying

Although it can be dried following the method for drying leaves in the section on Preservation, it is better to follow this traditional method. Spread the seaweed out on grass for several days to allow sun and rain showers to dry and bleach it. When dry and crisp, it is ready to store in a cardboard box with a lid, or in a brown paper bag tied with string. Stored in a cool dark place it will keep for a year or more.

Wild Carrageen and Wild Prawn Bisque

WILD CARRAGEEN AND
WILD PRAWN BISQUE

WHAT GOES IN

300g wild prawn shells

10g wild carrageen, dried

2 sticks organic celery

2 organic carrots, sliced

1 tbsp fennel seeds

1 large organic onion, sliced

2 organic cloves of garlic, sliced

½ an organic red chilli, chopped

2 bay leaves

2 sprigs of thyme

1 tbsp organic tomato purée

200ml organic white wine

2 litres fish stock

60ml organic cream

Organic olive oil, sea salt and freshly ground black pepper

HOW IT GOES

In a roasting tray, combine prawn shells, celery, carrot and fennel seeds, pour over some olive oil, mix. Roast for 20 minutes at 190°C.

Heat some olive oil in a large pot, put in the onion and cook until soft and golden, add the garlic, chilli, bay and thyme and cook for a further few minutes. Add in the tomato purée and cook for 3 to 4 minutes.

Add in the roasted prawn-shell mixture and the carrageen, stir together over the heat until everything is well mixed.

Then add the white wine and cook until reduced by half; finally pour in the fish stock and bring to the boil.

HOW TO FINISH

Turn the heat down and simmer for about 40–50 minutes. Blitz in a processor and strain back into a clean pot. Pour in cream, season with some salt and pepper to taste.

WHAT YOU GET

Is one of those double-whammy recipes … we like these! You have, quite obviously already indulged in a dinner of the peeled prawns; now rather than chucking the shells straight into the bin, you get yourself a prawn bisque that can be frozen, to enjoy for another time.

CARRAGEEN JELLY

From cottage to castle the classic Irish traditional recipe for carrageen is called variously carrageen jelly, carrageen blancmange and, occasionally, carrageen moss pudding, and in France *Mousse Irlandaise*.

7g dried carrageen, or as much as will fit in one's fist when almost closed
1 litre whole milk
30g sugar
1 egg
A vanilla pod, or ½ tsp vanilla essence

Soak the carrageen in tepid water for ten minutes. Put in a saucepan with the milk and vanilla pod. Bring to simmering point and simmer very gently for 20 minutes. Place a strainer over a bowl and rub the carrageen (which by now will be swollen and exuding jelly) through the strainer into the bowl and beat into the milk, adding the sugar, the vanilla essence (if using) and the yolk of the egg. (Test for a set as one would with gelatine). Whisk the egg white stiffly and fold gently into the mixture. It will rise to make a fluffy top. Serve with a fruit compote or a caramel of Irish coffee sauce.

Additions such as chopped ginger, grated lemon, or orange rind are traditional flavourings.

CHOWDER WITH DILLISK AND CARRAGEEN

600g fresh pollock or similar inshore fish, skinned and cubed

500g shellfish (mix of mussels, cockles, clams, winkles, prawns)

125g hot-smoked fish (eg pollock, haddock or mackerel), skinned and cubed

50g smoked dry cured bacon, cut into lardoons

30g butter

7g dried dillisk

7g dried carrageen

500ml fish stock or water

600ml milk (or milk and cream mixed)

1kg mixed vegetables in equal quantities (waxy potatoes, onion, leek, carrot, celery), peeled and finely chopped

A handful of chopped parsley, or parsley and chives mixed

Lightly cook and peel the prawns if using (or peel them while raw). Scrub clean the shellfish.

Cook bacon in butter until crisp; add all the vegetables except the potatoes. Season and cook over a gentle heat for 4–5 minutes. Add stock or water and the crumbled seaweeds and simmer for about 10 minutes. Add the potatoes and milk and simmer until potatoes are soft. You may set it aside at this point and finish off just before serving.

Add the cubed fish and shellfish and cook for a couple of minutes, stirring. Serve with plenty of chopped herbs. Good with dillisk-flavoured bread, scones, or oatcakes.

Wild Garlic

Allium ursinum * Irish *creamh*

There are many different types of wild garlic. Ramsom is the most widespread, common in traditional food culture. The flowers and leaves have a robust garlic flavour and many culinary uses.

WHERE TO LOOK

Wild garlic is a common plant and thrives in mixed woodlands and damp, shady places like country lanes and near streams.

WHAT IT LOOKS LIKE

Growing from a small, translucent bulb, pointed broad leaves push up through the soil, forming a multi-leaved bunch, followed by a single flower stalk bearing many small, white blossoms. The flower is highly identifiable (before it appears the plant might be mistaken for Lily of the Valley, which is poisonous). Wild garlic leaves have individual green-coloured stems; Lily of the Valley has a single purple stem. Another sure-fire identifying method is to grind the leaves between your fingers; they will produce a pungent, garlic-like aroma. Although local conditions or an early or late spring make harvesting time vary, in most years the time to gather is mid-March to mid-April and lasts for a month in any one location.

HOW TO PICK

Although the bulbs are edible, in the interest of sustainability you should not dig up bulbs, or strip the plant of all its leaves or flowers. Choose mid- to large-sized leaves and flower heads in blossom. Baskets are ideal for gathering. Pack loosely or you may bruise the leaves and flowers. Some people prefer the milder flavour the leaves have before flowering; others value a strong flavour and harvest leaves and flowers at the same time.

HOW TO PREPARE

Shake the flowers to remove insects. Wash flowers and leaves in cold water. Spread out on a clean cloth to remove moisture.

TRADITIONAL USES

The early Celts appreciated wild garlic so much that annual wild garlic feasts had to be provided by the lower orders for their chiefs and kings. In 1188 Gerard of Wales wrote of a 'fish sauce of wild garlic and butter for those of strong constitution'. The Irish Brehon Law tracts (in use in Ireland from two and a half thousand years ago to until nearly the end of the sixteenth century) define the amount of garlic to be served as a relish as four stalks to each loaf of bread. It is widely used in salads, as a pot herb with fish, to flavour soups, stews, potato dishes, breads, scones, savoury pies and tarts. As a medicine it was mixed with honey for coughs, colds and chest complaints.

PRESERVING WILD GARLIC

Leaves and flowers may be preserved in honey, oil, pickles and chutneys, or by drying following the method described in the Preservation section. When using in chutney or pickles, use whole or chopped leaves, added very close to the end of the cooking time.

Wild garlic lends itself best to preservation in oil – olive or rapeseed oil are the best choices.

You may use whole leaves, or blitz in a processor and pack into a sterilised Kilner jar, cover with oil and seal for future use. In temperate climates wild garlic pesto has become a modern classic, the leaves replacing both basil and garlic used in the original pesto of traditional Italian food culture.

Wild Garlic, Leek and Potato Bake with Wild Garlic Pesto.

WILD GARLIC, LEEK AND POTATO BAKE

WHAT GOES IN

30 leaves of fresh wild garlic, roughly chopped

125ml organic chicken or vegetable stock

150ml carton of organic cream

150ml organic milk

A knob of organic butter

Sea salt and freshly ground black pepper

2 organic leeks, thinly sliced

175g real ham, chopped

500g last year's organic potatoes peeled, sliced thinly

90g organic cheddar, grated

HOW IT GOES

Pour the stock, cream and milk into a small saucepan and bring to the boil. Season well.

Butter a one-litre gratin dish. Layer the potatoes, leeks and ham together in the dish, and spread out in even layers with the chopped wild garlic leaves. Pour over the seasoned liquid. Cover with foil and bake for 40 minutes at 180°C.

HOW TO FINISH

Remove the foil, sprinkle with the cheese and bake for another

30–40 minutes, spooning stock over occasionally, until the pota-toes are tender.

WHAT YOU GET
Well, the perfect accompaniment to a Sunday roast chicken, or as the first touch of spring to the last of the winter spuds or a great TV snack, when you have the munchies …

WILD GARLIC PESTO

WHAT GOES IN

  50g fresh wild garlic leaves

  25g pine, cashew, hazel or chestnuts

  … your choice!

  200ml organic olive oil or better still

  Irish organic rapeseed oil

  40g Parmigiano-Reggiano or really

  mature Desmond, grated

  Organic black pepper and sea salt.

HOW IT GOES
Simple recipes are not always the easiest. It's taken us years to get this just right. Any of the above nuts, oils or cheeses will make a fabulous fresh spring-tasting pesto … we're just not saying exactly which go into our Strawberry Tree wild garlic pesto!

So, the easy way is to blitz the nuts and half the oil in a food processor and add in the grated cheese. Then add the wild garlic and blitz with the remaining oil to the right consistency. Then simply season, to your taste. As a fresh oil dressing, it'll work, every time

HOW TO FINISH

Pour into sterilised Kilner jars and keep in the fridge or a really cool, dark pantry. More so than with basil pesto, there is a reaction between the wild garlic, oil and especially metal lids … hence the Kilner.

WHAT YOU GET

Is a serious pesto; a deep dark green pesto with attitude, a pesto that will slap you in the face with the unmistakably strong taste of wild natural garlic and its lush woodland dwellings. What you also get is 'bottled spring and summer' … to give as a present to your friends, if you are able!

If not, use it to impress as a dressing over salads, bake into your favourite bread dough, add to any pasta dish or mix with butter and slip under the skin of a chicken roast … the list goes on, just use your imagination and go wild!

WILD GARLIC PRESERVED IN OIL

An essential savoury preserve for the winter kitchen that you will find in many of the recipes in this book from flavouring salad dressings to adding zip to savoury tarts, soups and sauces.

Enough prepared wild garlic leaves to almost fill 4 250ml Kilner-type jars holding
1 litre of olive or rape seed oil

You may use whole leaves, or blitz in a processor. Pack into a sterilised, wide-necked Kilner-type jar, cover with the oil, pressing down a few times to eliminate any air bubbles present. Cover and seal and store in a cool dark place. Once opened, store in a refrigerator. If you are using just a little from the jar, press the leaves down again and top up with oil so that they are completely covered.

Any oil remaining, after you have used all the leaves, makes a delicious garlic-flavoured oil for using in a variety of recipes.

Wild Sea Beet

Beta vulgaris * Irish *biatas fiáin na mara*

Maritime sea beet or, as some call it, sea spinach, is a native wild plant along most European coasts. It is the wild ancestor of many cultivated vegetables, including beetroot, spinach, Swiss chard and sugar beet. For thousands of years many food cultures have used the tasty leaves as a food for humans and sometimes animals.

A perennial plant which flowers in summer, it is hermaphroditic and is wind pollinated. Salt tolerant, it thrives in full sun, in moist but well-drained conditions. The leaves taste similar to cultivated varieties with the addition of the tangy taste of the sea.

WHERE TO LOOK

Widespread on rocky and shingle seashores, sea cliffs, and close to such shores.

WHAT IT LOOKS LIKE

A spreading plant. The stems can grow up to a metre high. On each single stalk grows an oval-shaped, thick, waxy, shiny, dark green leaf. The flowers are greenish clusters of fleshy fruit with no petals. The thickness of the leaves means it retains a pleasing texture and does not 'cook down' nearly as much as cultivated varieties.

HOW TO PICK

Sea beet is a perennial that never dies back completely. It may be gathered as soon as the fresh leaves appear which, depending on the location and harshness of the weather, may emerge as early as late winter and continue growing and producing new leaves until halted by flowering sometime between July and late September. It can be treated as a 'cut-and-come-again' plant. Regular cropping encourages new leaves and discourages flowering and plants picked regularly until late October will go on producing leaves right into November. Pick the large leaves, leaving the very small leaves to grow on. Late in the season when flowers do appear they should be allowed to develop.

HOW TO PREPARE

Wash in cold water to remove sand. Any particularly thick stalks are best removed and use for stock or soup.

TRADITIONAL USES

Sea beet is traditionally eaten fresh and used exactly as spinach or chard – lightly blanched, or stir-fried and eaten as a salad; with crisp bacon; as a hot vegetable dish with melted butter or a little cream and nutmeg; in soups, stews, savoury tarts; as a filling for an omelette and for crêpes. It is particularly good with fish.

PRESERVING WILD SEA BEET

Because sea beet is available for such a long season it is normally eaten fresh. There is no great store of ways of preserving it for winter use. The best way of preserving it is to blanch the leaves in fast-boiling water until tender. Drain well and dry off on kitchen paper. Then pack the leaves into sterilised jars and cover with oil, pressing it well down to get rid of air bubbles and making sure the oil comes close to the top of the jar. Cover with a tight lid and store in a cool dark place.

WILD SEA BEET AND WILD CRAB TART

WHAT GOES IN

Two handfuls of sea beet, stalks removed, leaves washed, roughly chopped

300g fresh wild crabmeat

1 organic onion, finely chopped

2 garlic cloves, crushed and chopped

1 red chilli, deseeded and finely chopped

Wild Sea Beet and Wild Crab Tart.

1 bunch coriander, roughly chopped

Juice of one lemon

50g Parmesan, grated

250ml organic cream

4 organic egg yolks, plus 1 whole egg

Sea salt and pepper

Organic olive oil

Your favourite recipe for savoury pastry, blind baked
in a 20-22cm tart dish

HOW IT GOES

In a large frying pan, fry onions until soft. Then add chilli, garlic
and fry for a few more minutes. Add the sea beet, and when soft,
toss in the crabmeat. Fry together and mix thoroughly, then add
the coriander, lemon juice and Parmesan.

Lightly beat together the egg and cream and season.

HOW TO FINISH

Spoon the sea beet mixture into your baked tart case. Pour over
your egg and cream. Bake, for 30–40 minutes at 140°C, or until
set.

WHAT YOU GET

Is a quiche-style seafood pie that oozes the sea and that can be
served cold, warm or hot, all the way through the summer. We
like to serve it warm, with a baby leaf salad and mayonnaised
baby new potatoes.

SEA BEET, SULTANAS AND CREAM GRATIN

500g sea beet leaves, stalks removed, washed and chopped

2 tbsp butter

60–90ml cream

2 tbsp sultanas

¼ tsp freshly ground nutmeg

2–3 chopped leaves of wild garlic, optional

2–3 tablespoons Glebe Brethan or similar Gruyère-type cheese

Place prepared sea beet in a pot. Half cover with boiling water and cook for 2–3 minutes, or until tender. Drain and chop. Heat the butter in a pan and stir-fry the chopped sea beet for a minute. If you wish to use sea beet preserved in oil simply remove excess oil with kitchen paper and chop finely.

Add the cream to the chopped sea beet, sultanas, and nutmeg; season with black pepper. Place in a gratin dish. Top with grated cheese. Bake at 190°C for about 15 minutes, or until piping hot through and the cheese topping is golden. Serve hot with pretty well any main dish from grilled or roast lamb or beef, or bacon, to fish and shellfish.

Wild Rock Samphire

Crithmum maritimum * Irish *cabáiste aille*

Wild rock samphire is a native plant, common in Europe on Atlantic coasts and the shores of the Mediterranean. It is one of a kind, being the only species in the genus *Crithmum*. In Donegal the local name 'passper' comes from the French *perce-pierre*, meaning 'pierce rock', well named for the plant seems to grow from rock not soil. Nor is it fussy about the type of rock; the chalk cliffs of Dover may have prompted Shakespeare's line in *King Lear*, 'Half-way down hangs one that gathered samphire; dreadful trade!'

There is no need to risk life and limb. It also grows on rocky and shingle beeches. The narrow leaves have a fleshy, almost succulent structure. It has a particular affinity to fish and seafood with a pungent aroma rather like aniseed.

WHERE TO LOOK

At the upper end of seashores with rock outcrops or shingle, especially those that have suffered coastal erosion and cliff falls. It has colonised dry-stone seawalls, even those built in recent times.

WHAT IT LOOKS LIKE

It is quite short, from 16–40cm, and clings around the rock.

From a woody base the stems keep dividing and producing narrow leaves that are bright mid-green in colour, getting darker as the season progresses. The multi-headed flowers are a greenish-yellow which, if the plant is not harvested, emerge as early as July.

HOW TO PICK

Harvesting begins in early March. You can cut the narrow leaves with a scissors or nip off with your nails (if they are reasonably long). It's a cut-and-come-again plant. Early in the year, the more you harvest, the more leaves grow, within reason. Choose middle- to large-sized leaves, allowing the smaller ones to grow on. In good conditions you can harvest through to September or later, as long as you leave some stems on the plant to flower.

HOW TO PREPARE

Wash in cold water and drain. Pick over carefully and discard any wind-browned leaves. It will keep fresh for a couple of days in a fridge. However, if you are going to preserve it, it is best to do this as soon as is practical.

TRADITIONAL USES

Eaten in ancient Greece and Rome. The taste is too strong for eating raw and traditionally it was boiled briefly and served with melted butter as a hot vegetable to accompany or garnish seafood, or to enhance the flavour of soups, particularly chowder, as well as fish pies, risotto, and pasta dishes. In Wales it is served with salt marsh lamb and mutton. Pickled samphire was well known as a salad accompaniment to shellfish and cold cuts of game, like wild duck, and with cheese – particularly blue cheeses.

PRESERVING WILD ROCK SAMPHIRE

Pickling is the only method of preserving samphire in common use.

Plunge prepared rock samphire into fast-boiling water for a minute, or two if the leaves are thick. Drain in a large colander and cool quickly under cold running water. Shake dry and spread on a clean cloth to absorb any remaining water. Pack into wide-necked, sterilised jars.

Boil white wine or cider vinegar with spices of your choice and pour over the samphire so that it is completely covered. Seal and store in a cool, dark place.

PICKLED WILD ROCK SAMPHIRE

WHAT GOES IN

500g wild rock samphire

300g organic caster sugar

Small organic onion, sliced finely

1 organic celery stick, chopped finely

2 organic bay leaves

½ tsp organic pink peppercorns

½ tsp organic fennel seeds

1 tsp organic mustard seeds

½ organic red chilli – chopped finely

Zest of 1 lemon

500ml organic red wine vinegar

HOW IT GOES

Twice wash the wild rock samphire and set aside in a large container. In a large pot, place sugar, onion, celery, bay, seeds, chilli, lemon zest and pour over the vinegar. Put on the heat and stir until everything is mixed. Bring to boil and then simmer for a few minutes. Let cool a bit, then pour the pickle over the rock samphire in the large container.

HOW TO FINISH

Pack the warm rock samphire into sterilised Kilner jars, then pour in the strained pickle, filling the jar right to the top. Put the lids back on and it will keep up to 3 months in a cool, dark place.

WHAT YOU GET

Pickled samphire works well with all shellfish, but it is also perfect to keep for when flatfish are caught after September. It is also a treat with honky-heady Irish blue cheese or really well-matured Irish hard cheeses and, finally, is a cool pickle that works really well with slow-cooked winter Irish Hill Hogget.

FRESH MACKEREL PIE WITH FRESH WILD ROCK SAMPHIRE

4 fresh mackerel, boned

100g fresh rock samphire, prepared, and lightly blanched.

1 onion, chopped

1 leek, chopped

1 sweet red or orange pepper, deseeded and cut into 10cm square pieces

4 tbsp wild garlic, preserved in oil, chopped

700g fluffy mashed potatoes

100ml fish stock

50ml dry white wine or cider

90ml cream

2 tbsp butter, or oil from the wild garlic

Place the mackerel fillets in a large wide pan and poach very lightly in the fish stock. Remove skin if wished, and cool. Soften the onion, leek, and sweet pepper in butter or wild garlic oil. Spread equal amounts on the bottom of 4 fish-sized gratin dishes. Open fillets out and stuff with wild garlic leaves and season with sea salt and black pepper. Fold closed and place on top of the vegetables. Place sprigs of the wild samphire on top of the fish. Deglaze the vegetable pan with the wine or cider and bubble up to reduce.

Add the fish stock and bubble up. Next add the cream and continue cooking until it is reduced to a pleasing slightly thickened consistency. Pour over the fish and vegetables. Spread the fluffy mashed potatoes on top and draw a fork over to create shallow ridges. Bake at 190°C for about 10–15 minutes, or until it is piping hot all the way through to the centre of the fish and the potato topping is pleasingly crisp and golden. Serve hot with a leaf salad enlivened with wild leaves and flower blossoms on the side.

Wild St George's Mushroom

Calocybe gambosa * Irish *beacán naomh seoirse*

Currently named *Calocybe gambosa* (the original Latin name came from a slang term for a club foot because it has a bulky stem). The official name has been reclassified three times! It acquired its common name because it first appears around the feast day of St George on 23 April. It grows all over Europe. Highly prized for its flavour and its affinity to butter and the fact that it appears in spring when fungi are scarce. It has a habit of forming vast 'fairy rings'. One in the south of England is so huge it is thought to be hundreds of years old.

WHERE TO LOOK

On grasslands, pasture, the margins of woodlands, grass roadside verges, often in areas that are rich in limestone.

WHAT IT LOOKS LIKE

The convex cap can be as small as 5cm and as large as 15cm in diameter. The cap, flesh and stem (which is bulky at the base)

run from creamy white to bright yellow and the gills are white, narrow, and crowded close together and the flesh is white, thick and soft. The aroma is mealy with a whiff of cucumber. Other mushrooms that grow in the same habitat, which are not edible, have a different smell, either a pungent, fruity or rancid aroma or flesh that bruises red if squashed.

HOW TO PICK

Choose a dry day and bring a basket and a small sharp knife with a long slim blade or a mushroom knife. Pick by cutting across the base. Choose medium-sized mushrooms, leaving the smaller ones for another day to grow. Leave old, over-large ones to spread their spores.

HOW TO PREPARE

Check the identity of each one. Cut off the earthy base. Do not peel or you will lose the flavour. Wipe with a clean cloth or damp kitchen paper. All fungi should be eaten or preserved without delay.

TRADITIONAL USES

St George's are delicious simply fried in fresh butter and eaten hot. A welcome element of a cooked breakfast with bacon, eggs, puddings and sausage. Also traditionally used in soups, sauces, stuffings and savoury tarts. Older, darker ones were usually preserved as a ketchup and used in winter as a flavouring, either pickled, or dried for later use.

PRESERVING WILD ST GEORGE'S MUSHROOMS

In recipes mushrooms are usually interchangeable. Mushrooms may be preserved in oil, pickled and dried. Details of the methods may be found in the Preservation section.

WILD ST GEORGE'S MUSHROOM, SPINACH AND GORGONZOLA RISOTTO

WHAT GOES IN

200g of organic spinach, shredded

300g St George's mushrooms

2 organic onions, peeled and finely chopped

2 organic garlic cloves, finely chopped

1 organic leek, finely chopped

30ml organic olive oil

350g organic risotto rice

1¼ litres organic stock (chicken or vegetable)

60g freshly grated, Parmesan

90g organic butter

50g Gorgonzola cheese

Sea salt and freshly ground black pepper

HOW IT GOES

Rip the stalks from the spinach leaves. Wash and drain well. Remove any dirt from the mushrooms and brush or wipe them clean, then cut them into small, less than bite-size pieces. Fry the mushrooms in a pan for 2–3 minutes and leave aside.

For the risotto, heat the olive oil in a pan and gently sauté the onion, leek and garlic until translucent, add the rice and stir well with a wooden spoon. Gradually add the stock, a little at a time,

stirring constantly and ensuring that the stock has been absorbed each time before adding more. It will take about 15 minutes.

When the rice is nearly cooked, add the spinach, mushrooms and Parmesan.

HOW TO FINISH
Add a little more stock and finish with the butter and the Gorgonzola. The risotto should be quite moist. Season with sea salt, freshly ground black pepper and top with a little more Parmesan.

WHAT YOU GET
We all know that mushroom risotto is the biz and works really well. However, it will never reach the same level as a risotto made with wild mushrooms.

SPICY MUSHROOM POWDER

This condiment is wonderful for adding the aroma and flavour of wild mushrooms to soups, stews, sauces, or extra flavour to cultivated mushrooms. Ideal when you come across a large flush of mushrooms.

    1kg large St George's mushrooms, prepared and sliced
    1 large onion, finely chopped
    2–4 blades of mace (or 1 tbsp ground mace)
    5 cloves
    1 tsp freshly ground black pepper

Place all the ingredients on a wide pan and cook gently until the juices from the mushrooms begin to run. Raise the heat and, stirring all the time, cook until the juices have been absorbed by the onions and spices.

Spread out on a baking tray and place in an oven at 80–100°C. Keep an eye that they do not burn. When they are completely dry blitz to a powder in a food processor. Spoon into a glass jar with an airtight lid.

ST GEORGE'S MUSHROOM AND POTATO GRATIN WITH WILD GARLIC

350g St George's mushrooms, prepared and sliced thinly
700g potatoes, choose a waxy or new early season potatoes
1 large clove of garlic, peeled, crushed and finely chopped, or
4–5 leaves wild garlic, chopped
300ml cream
2 tbsp water
1–2 tbsp butter
4 tbsp Parmesan cheese, or very well-aged Cheddar or
Gruyère cheese, grated
Sea salt and freshly ground black pepper

Peel or scrape new potatoes and slice thinly. Rub half the butter all over the inside of a gratin dish or individual ramekins. Starting with the potatoes, build up layers of potato, mushroom and garlic. Season each layer with salt and pepper as you go.

Stir the water into the cream and pour over the layers. Sprinkle the cheese over the top. Bake at 150–160°C for about 1–1½ hours, or until the potatoes are tender and the top is crisp.

Sheep Sorrel

Wild Sorrel

Rumex acetosella (sheep sorrel) * Irish *samhadh caorach*
Oxalis acetosella (wood sorrel) * Irish *seamsóg*

There are a number of types of wild sorrel, including sheep sorrel (*Rumex acetosella*) with broad leaves and the three-leaved wood sorrel (*Oxalis acetosella*). They look different and are found in different locations. However, known as cooling plants, they share a sour, lemony flavour and both were once used much as lemons are today. They have scores of common names, many reflecting the sour flavour or the animals that favour them for grazing like cuckoo bread, fox bread, hare's meat, bird's bread and cheese, sheep sorrel, wood sour, and 'Whitsun flower' relating to the season when you would expect to see it bloom. In parts of England it is known simply as 'green sauce' after the popular sauce made with the leaves.

WHERE TO LOOK

Sheep sorrel grows on grassland and open places on roadsides, ditches and gardens. Wood sorrel flourishes in woodland and hedge bottoms.

WHAT IT LOOKS LIKE

Sheep sorrel has soft smooth spinach-like leaves between 7–26cm

Note the arrow shape at the base of the sheep sorrel leaf.

long, mid-green in colour and with a thin, creamy central stalk on each leaf and rusty-reddish flower spikes. It can grow up to 50–60 cm high.

Wood sorrel is low-growing with multiple three-leaved sprigs that open and fold down in response to light and dark and rain. Delicate pinkish-white flowers can be seen from May to August. The leaves can be harvested from early spring to late autumn.

HOW TO PICK

Pick sheep sorrel one leaf at a time, leaving the immature leaves to grow on. Pick three-leaved wood sorrel one sprig at a time.

HOW TO PREPARE

Rinse under cold, running water, tearing away any blemished leaves as you rinse. Cut off the stalks and any larger ribs of sheep sorrel (do this by folding the leaf in two and ripping gently from the end of the stalk). Shake dry, spread out and allow the moisture to evaporate.

TRADITIONAL USES

Sorrel is available over a long season so it is not surprising that, traditionally, it was used fresh in salads, soups, as a hot vegetable, to add flavour to stews and as a main ingredient in a variety of sauces. In Ireland wild salmon and wild sorrel sauce was a traditional combination. Many traditional European recipes, especially those from France, where it is particularly prized, reflect its affinity with eggs: omelettes, or poached or baked eggs, and also as a stuffing for fish.

Most famously in England preserved sorrel was used as a green sauce to serve with goose, fish, and roast or grilled meat, and to flavour stews. Alan Davidson writes in his *Oxford Companion to Food* of 'Green Sauce owing its colour to green leaves, especially sorrel. Something of the kind may well date back to classical times and was apparent in medieval cookery in various parts of Europe.'

PRESERVING WILD SORREL

Sorrel may be dried, preserved in oil, or chopped and mixed with vinegar and sugar. See the Preservation section.

When cooking with sorrel it is important not to use a non-stick surface as the chemicals react with the coating.

Pictured right: on top wood sorrel, below sheep sorrel growing from moss and fern.

WILD SHEEP SORREL SAUCE

WHAT GOES IN

100g wild sheep sorrel leaves, torn

1 organic onion, peeled and sliced

250ml organic white wine

400ml organic vegetable stock or fish
stock

250ml organic cream

Sea salt and freshly ground black pepper

HOW IT GOES

Wild sheep sorrel is best. However, you could mix in wood sorrel
for volume. Wash the sorrel leaves, leave to drain.

Heat a heavy-bottomed pan and add a little olive oil. Sauté the
onion until soft. Add the white wine and bring to the boil. Pour
in the stock and cook until reduced by half, add the cream. Cook
again until reduced by half. Remove from the heat, add the sorrel
leaves and blitz with a hand blender.

HOW TO FINISH

Just 'season to taste' and it's good to go! We like it this way, with
small pieces of fresh wild sorrel through it. However, if you like it
smoother, simply pass it through a sieve.

WHAT YOU GET

This brilliant, bright, tart green sauce is great to serve with any 'shrimp-induced' pink fish like salmon or sea trout. Simply steam the fish and pour the sauce over. Works really well with poached shellfish also. Sorry, this works well with any fish!

GREEN SAUCE

This method of preserving sorrel has been used for hundreds of years. Used as a sauce with meat and poultry, particularly fatty meats like lamb, pork, goose and duck.

250g sorrel leaves, rinsed, ribs and stems removed
Lemon juice or wine vinegar
Sugar

Blanch sorrel in boiling water. Pound to a paste in a mortar and pestle with lemon juice and sugar. If you prefer, use a food processor, adding juice and sugar with the sorrel aids the process. You will end up with something resembling preserved mint sauce. Pack into sterilised glass jars, cover tightly and store in a cool dry place.

You need a fair amount of sugar and lemon juice/vinegar in order for this to keep. To serve, add a little boiling water to thin the consistency and make the preserve less sour and acid.

WILD SORREL TABBOULEH

250g fine bulgur wheat

4–5 tbsp virgin olive oil or rapeseed oil, or to taste

4 scallions, finely chopped

8 leaves of fresh sheep sorrel, or 20 leaves of fresh wood sorrel, or sorrel preserved in olive or rapeseed oil, or four dried sheep sorrel leaves reconstituted in a small quantity of water (or water and lemon juice mixed)

8 tbsp parsley, chopped

2 tbsp wild mint, chopped

Lemon juice, to taste

Salt and freshly ground black pepper

A few cherry tomatoes

Pour enough boiling water over the bulgur wheat to cover, plus a little extra; allow to sit until cool. Drain and squeeze out any excess water and mix bulgur wheat with the chopped scallions, sorrel, parsley, mint, and oil and season with the salt and pepper. Add lemon juice to taste. Top with tomatoes.

Note: Other ingredients such as sweet peppers and olives may be added as you wish.

Wild Hawthorn

Crataegus monogyna * Irish *sceach gheal*

A member of the Rosaceae family, the haw tree grows wild all over Europe and beyond and probably has more local names than any other native tree: whitethorn, quickthorn, the bread and cheese tree and, when in flower, the May, the May bush and the Mayflower. The flower forms a wonderful foam of white and since Celtic times has been the flower of The Spring Festival, marking the start of the farming year – in Irish *Lá Bealtaine*. In Irish folklore May Eve and May Day is a time when the *sidhe*, the fairies, are about, as excited as humans at the coming of new milk and butter and liable to steal farm produce for themselves – one reason why people left lone hawthorns for the fairies. Whatever about the flowers, the buds are a tasty wayside nibble and, despite a belief which grew up that the haw berries gave you jaundice, they have many uses both culinary and medicinal.

WHERE TO LOOK

A native tree used as a stockproof hedgerow plant; it is the most abundant of all wild fruit plants and in autumn turns many farm lanes and country roadsides bright red.

WHAT IT LOOKS LIKE

It is a many-branched, small tree, often knarled and twisted as they can live for a hundred years. The thorns and the long leaves which grow on short shoots vary in the size and shape of their lobes which can number between 3 and 7. Flowers are white or pink and grow in clusters about 2cm wide; the fruit, or haw, is 1cm wide, bright red with a single stone seed within.

HOW TO PICK

You will need long sleeves and gloves and a walking-stick to hook down taller branches. In early spring, some of the youngest leaves and flower buds can be nipped off the branch. The flower heads, once they are fully in bloom, can be picked. The berries can be picked in clusters and allowed to drop into a bucket.

HOW TO PREPARE BUDS AND BERRIES

Spread the flowers or berries on a work surface; discard leaves, stalks and any tired-looking flowers and the occasional insect.

Shake the flowers and roll the berries on a clean cloth just to be sure and, if you feel you must, give them a quick rinse in cold water and dry on clean towels or kitchen paper. Buds and blossoms should be used while fresh and not wilted. The berries will last a few days in a cool place without coming to harm.

TRADITIONAL USES

Hawthorn buds are a tasty wayside nibble and, along with hawthorn leaves, are added to salads.

Hawthorn flowers were prized for their strong almond-scent and made into wine and a flavoured liqueur.

The berries were never eaten raw but were often fermented into wine. They make a tasty syrup. A mixture of haws and a small amount of crab apples were made into delicately flavoured jelly that is a great accompaniment to cream cheese. Their most common use was in 'hedgerow jam' made from a mixture of autumn berries.

PRESERVING HAWS

The blossoms can be added to alcohol and can be drunk straight away. Berry-flavoured spirits are best drunk after a few months.

Pack a Kilner-type jar with fresh blossoms. Cover with whiskey or brandy. Strain after about two weeks. Add sugar or strong sugar syrup if needed.

Drying haws is different to the usual methods for berries. Spread the berries on a baking tray and dry in an oven set to 50°C for one hour. Cool and repeat for 3–6 days until fully dried. Store, covered, in a jar or box in a very dry place.

Haws in jams and jellies are mixed with crab apple as haws on their own are rather dry. The proportion of one quarter crab apple to haws is usual in order not to swamp the flavour of the haws. Again because of their dryness, a lot of berries are needed for wine. It takes 2kg of berries to make 4½ litres of wine. For jams, jelly, wine and syrups follow the instructions described in the Preservation section.

INIS TURK DELIGHTS
OF WILD HAWTHORN
FLOWER AND POITÍN

WHAT GOES IN

1 cup of wild haw flowers

20g leaf gelatine

700g granulated sugar

130g cornflour

30g icing sugar

A few drops of rose water

Juice of two lemons

300ml water

3 tbsp *poitín* or vodka

HOW IT GOES

Soak the gelatine leaves in a shallow dish of cold water. In a heavy-based pan, heat gently and dissolve the sugar in lemon juice in 200ml of water. In a bowl, mix 100g of cornflour in 100ml of water until smooth; take the pan off the heat and stir cornflour mixture into the sugar syrup. Return the pan to a low heat.

Squeeze the gelatine to remove excess water, and then add it and the haw flowers to the mixture and whisk until the gelatine has dissolved. Bring the mixture very slowly to the boil and simmer for 15 minutes, stirring almost constantly.

Remove once the mixture has clarified and become 'gloopy'. Stir in the *poitín* and the rose water and leave to cool for 10 minutes.

Inis Turk Delights of Wild Hawthorn Flower and Poitín.

Mix 30g of cornflour with the icing sugar, to make a 'dusting powder'.

Line a shallow baking tin with baking parchment, fill with mixture and dust.

HOW TO FINISH

Leave in a cool place until set. Once cooled, place in the fridge for a few hours until it becomes slightly rubbery. Cut the Inis Turk Delight into cubes with a knife and dust with the remaining dusting agent. It should keep in the fridge for 3–4 weeks.

WHAT YOU GET

Some of us remember the treat of Turkish Delight at Christmas. This is our x-rated adult version! Homage is to Inis Turk and makes absolutely no reference to *poitín* that might or might not come from in or around that location. Inis Turk Delight works a treat at the end of dinner with a musky dessert wine.

HAWTHORN BLOSSOM AND BRANDY LIQUEUR

Enough blossom to almost fill a ¾-litre Kilner jar, prepared
4 tbsp icing sugar
1 bottle brandy

Remove every piece of even the smallest stem and pack the flower heads in the jar shaking them down but taking care not to bruise the flowers. Shake the icing sugar over the flowers. Fill up the jar with the brandy and cover tightly. Place in a warm dark cupboard. For the first few weeks shake a few times a week to help the sugar to dissolve fully. Then store in a dark place for 3 months. When it matures, strain to remove the blossom and bottle the liqueur. It is now ready to drink or use as a flavouring for desserts and sweet sauces.

Wild Elderflower

Sambucus nigra (elder) *Irish *bláththroim* (elderflower)

Elder is one of a number of indigenous, shrub-like trees that became common about six thousand years ago following forest clearance by the first farmers. The Celts accorded the elder with magic qualities and flowers and berries were symbols of the agricultural year. White blossom was a sign of spring and the purplish-black berries a sign of fulfilment of the harvest and renewed life. In old Irish Brehon law texts *trom* (the elder) is in the list of third-class trees. As the wood itself has no practical use, its classification probably was because it was prized for its aromatic blossoms and juicy berries.

WHERE TO LOOK

Elder is a common tree all over Europe. You will find it in hedgerows, beside footpaths, in neglected and recently cleared woodland, parks and gardens.

WHAT IT LOOKS LIKE

Elder is an untidy, many-stemmed, shrub tree rarely more than 5 metres high; the bark is corky and grey-white in colour; it has 5–7

elliptical, finely-toothed, soft, green leaves. In spring it has bracks of white blossom. In late summer these turn into reddish clusters of small berries which, as they ripen, turn purple/black and, depending on aspect and altitude, are normally ready for picking in September.

HOW TO PICK

In roadside hedgerows the easy-to-reach branches have often been sheered back, leaving the best flowers at the top of the tree – a long hooked stick is handy to pull the braches down within reach. Elder blossom is carried on mature branches so if a hedge has been given a short top and sides all you will see is the regrowth of leaves. Take heart, many farmers only reduce hedges every second year.

HOW TO PREPARE

Choose a dry day when the dew has dried off. Harvest when newly in bloom and as far from traffic fumes as possible and avoiding elder trees that border land that is likely to have been sprayed with chemicals. Shake each flower head to get rid of insects and give it a quick rinse under running water.

TRADITIONAL USES

Flowers are used for making wines, vinegars, cordials, syrups and chutney and can be scattered over salads and used in fritters. A small branch of blossom is often used as an additional flavouring with fruit like gooseberries as it imparts a grape-like flavour. They are used to add flavour to and perfume tea breads and sweet scones and icecream. The flowers also are dried to make herb tea with a soothing quality. Elderflowers are also used to make a delicious elderflower 'champagne'.

PRESERVING WILD ELDERFLOWERS

Elderflowers can be sugared, preserved in oil, syrup, or vinegar, fermented into wine, and dried. Methods are described in the Preservation section.

Wild Elderflower Fritters.

WILD ELDERFLOWER FRITTERS

WHAT GOES IN

10 heads of wild elderflowers

1 organic egg

250ml organic rapeseed oil

150ml ice-cold water

1 tsp bicarbonate of soda

85g plain flour or 85g tempura flour

Sea salt

HOW IT GOES

Break the egg into a bowl containing the iced water and whisk until frothy. Add the soda and flour. Beat until the flour is just mixed in. The batter should be so thin that merely a wisp clings to the elderflowers when dipped in. If it seems too thick, add a little more iced water. Always keep the batter cold.

Heat oil, to a frying temperature 185–190°C. Dip each flower-head into the batter, lightly tapping on the side of the bowl to remove excess batter and then deep fry until golden in colour … seconds!

HOW TO FINISH

Drain on kitchen paper to remove excess fat, sprinkle with sea salt and serve at once.

WHAT YOU GET

Well, with the tempura flour it's light enough to impress your friends with a glass of bubbly. Salted, it goes great as a main course of spring vegetable with the last of the season's run of the Irish round fish … hake, haddock and more.

If you prefer a sweeter version to savoury, perhaps as an accompaniment to ice cream, well then, simply substitute fine sugar for the sea salt.

ELDERFLOWER CHAMPAGNE

10 heads of fresh or dried wild elderflowers

4 litres cold water

2 lemons

650g sugar

2 tbsp white wine vinegar

Dissolve sugar in a little warm water and allow to cool. Squeeze in the juice from the lemons. Put everything (including the lemon skins) into the fermentation container. Cover and infuse for 4 days. Strain off and bottle in screw-topped bottles. It should be ready to drink in 4 weeks but test after 1 week to see that it does not get too fizzy. Slightly unscrew all caps to release pressure for a small period of time. On the other hand, if it fails to work, leave it for another month; sometimes the natural yeast of the flowers is very slow to get going.

Wild Sea Lettuce

Ulva lactuca * Irish *leitís na farraige & glasán*

Wild sea lettuce so named because it looks a little like a lettuce leaf. Unlike many other edible seaweeds, it is tender and does not require cooking and has a terrific flavour similar to sorrel. It is easy to find, easy to identify and a popular sea vegetable in many food cultures of the world. Like all seaweeds it is nourishing as it is packed full of vitamins and minerals. It has a long season from spring to late autumn.

WHERE TO LOOK

Look just below the tide mark in rock pools and shallow waters and you'll find it pretty well anywhere along the shore growing from other seaweeds and rocks.

A seaweed that detaches easily from its holdfast, you will often see fronds washed up on the beach. Unless you can actually see them being stranded by an outgoing tide it is safer to gather them yourself.

WHAT IT LOOKS LIKE

Vivid bright-green, almost translucent. The size varies from 10–40cm long.

HOW TO PICK

Choose a clean uncontaminated shore. Remove the leaves by snipping from its holdfast with a scissors or small sharp knife and gather in a small child's sandcastle bucket or a plastic bag. Sea lettuce is rather lightly attached to its holdfast, so care is needed when picking.

HOW TO PREPARE

Wash in cold water to remove the sand and it is ready for use.

TRADITIONAL USES

Although tender enough to eat raw in salads, you may wish to blanch it briefly in fast boiling water, cooling it quickly before adding to salads. It is more often used in dressings, soups, sauces, stir-fries, and to add flavour to fish and shellfish dishes. It is particularly useful as an edible wrap for whole or filleted fish, and in a wide range of tasty fillings. In many food cultures it was lightly cooked and eaten as a hot vegetable.

PRESERVING WILD SEA LETTUCE

· ·

Drying

Sea lettuce may be dried (although it will lose its lovely colour), preserved as a pickle, or in oil.

Spread the cleaned fronds in one layer on a wire rack and leave in a sunny dry place until dried crisp. Alternately place rack in a very low oven or a dehydrator at 35–50°C and leave until dry. Store in brown paper bags in a dry, dark place.

In Brine

Pack cleaned fronds into a pottery jar. Pour over the brine or pickling solution of your choice. Several options and methods are outlined in the Preservation section.

WILD SEA LETTUCE LAVERBREADS

WHAT GOES IN

500g of fresh wild sea lettuce

150g organic porridge oatlets, or enough to bind the seaweed

6 slices of organic streaky bacon, chopped

2 tbsp Worcestershire sauce

1 tbsp organic tomato purée

1 organic egg

Organic black pepper

HOW IT GOES

Simmer the sea lettuce for 2 hours. Traditional recipes demanded 8–10 hours, but they did not have processors! Pour off excess liquid. After it has cooled, blitz in a processor with the streaky bacon, Worcestershire sauce, tomato purée and egg. Add enough oatlets to bind ingredients together. Season. Form into flat thick 'pattie'-style cakes, and cover all over with the remaining oatlets.

HOW TO FINISH

Fry, really, really slowly on a medium heat until cooked through, turning several times.

WHAT YOU GET

Is a great alternative to the usual traditional Irish Breakfast. Show off to your friends, if they stay over, by serving with soft eggs and mushrooms in the morning. Works really well, also, at dinner, with a simple pan-fried fillet of white fish and a fresh baby leaf salad.

CRAB MEAT AND SAMPHIRE WRAPPED IN SEA LETTUCE

350g cooked crab meat, preferably white and brown mixed
1 handful of wild rock samphire, lightly cooked or pickled, chopped
2 leaves wild garlic, chopped, or a large clove, finely chopped
3 tbsp double cream
About 12–16 fronds of sea lettuce

Pick over the crab meat and remove any pieces of shell. Place in a bowl and add the wild rock samphire, garlic and cream and season to taste with freshly ground black pepper. Form into little barrel shapes and wrap each shape in sea lettuce making sure there are no holes in the wrapping. Place in a steamer for about ten minutes or until hot through. Serve as an appetizer, or with a salad as a light lunch.

Wild Herbs and Flowers

. . . .

WILD THYME

. . . .

Thymus serphylum * Irish *lus na mbrat*

Wild thyme a common herb, particularly in limestone and chalk areas, on rocks and grasslands close to the sea such as the short-stemmed grass on the landward side of sand dunes, soil-topped stone banks, and similar dry places inland, on well-drained hills and mountains. Wild thyme is low growing and its dark-green aromatic leaves and mauve flowers have a gentler flavour than cultivated varieties. It flowers in summer. In most places it is an evergreen plant that can be picked all year round. Both leaves and flowers are edible. It responds well to drying and is a popular herb tea.

MINT

. . . .

Mentha * Irish *miontas*

At least a dozen different mints can be found in the wild. The aroma is readily recognised although they can look and taste

subtly different. They hybridise naturally and because they spread by underground roots that pop up all over the place, garden varieties have crept outwards and become naturalised. Most have green or greenish-purple leaves (some hairy and some shiny). They can be quite tall with large flower spikes any colour from white to deep purple. A perennial plant, mints have a long season, pushing up though the ground in early spring and only dying back when hard winter frosts start.

Look in dampish, moist places that get some sun. Water mint grows in really wet places and usually has a strong flavour. Mints are used to flavour everything from toothpaste to cocktails, sauces and jelly. They can be dried or preserved with sugar, with or without added vinegar.

MEADOWSWEET

* *

Filipendula ulmaria * Irish *airgead luachra*

Abundant in all country areas, on damp roadway hedgerows, ditches, woodland and bogs, meadowsweet is easy to spot with long reddish-coloured stems often over a metre high. The flowers are large and cream in colour and there is a strong honey-sweet aroma unlike any other plant and herein lies its usefulness. It can replace sugar and honey in recipes and makes sweet flower tea. It is gorgeous added to a summer wine cup. The leaves are sharp tasting and can be used for a thirst-quenching drink.

WILD PRIMROSE & WILD SWEET VIOLET

• •

Primula vulgaris * Irish *sabhaircín* & *Viola odorata* * Irish *sail-chuach chumhra*

Low-growing, common and easily found in woodland, hedgerows, and banks in spring and summer time. Violet leaves are almost evergreen while the primrose dies back after flowering. A feature of both is that during their season the more you pick the more flowers grow. The leaves and flowers of both are edible and have a wonderful perfume. Use fresh to add

colour and flavour to salads, desserts and drinks. There is a long tradition of crystallising them for decorating cakes.

GORSE, FURZE, WHIN

* *

Ulex europaeus * Irish *aiteann gallda*

Call it what you will. A widespread shrub of hilly land, waste land and in some areas used as a stock-proof windproof hedgerow.

Green and thorny leaves and bright yellow blooms flowering most abundantly in spring. It carries some flowers all year round. The flavour is variously described as like almonds or coconut and it makes a tasty syrup, tea, or a flavoured liqueur.

WILD THYME AND ELDERBERRY SAUCE

225g fresh wild elderberries, stripped from stalk
A handful of wild thyme, chopped
A few tablespoons water, red wine, or port
Sugar to taste

Simmer the berries and thyme in your chosen liquid for a few minutes until just tender. Sweeten to taste. Perfect with game.

MINT JELLUP

A measure of whiskey
4 good-sized sprigs of fresh mint, chopped
10ml water

Bruise the mint leaves and water in a small glass. Add ice cubes and whiskey. Stir and enjoy.

MEADOWSWEET WITH A WILD BERRY COMPOTE

A neat and inexpensive way of getting a sweet, aromatic flavour similar to dessert wine. The meadowsweet supplies a honey-like sweetness.

350g mixed berries of your choice: wild strawberry, raspberry, bilberry, elderberry, blackberry
4 meadowsweet flower heads, fresh or dried, stalk removed
A glass of white wine

Place the berries, meadowsweet flowers and white wine in a stainless steel pot. Heat gradually until it reaches a simmering temperature. Remove from the heat and allow flavours to mingle. Serve with cream, crème fraiche, or porridge for breakfast.

CRYSTALLISED PRIMROSES OR VIOLETS

A labour of love, this recipe is for those with patience and steady hands. The result makes stunning decorations for cakes, desserts such as ice cream, syllabub, fruit salads and fruit tarts.

A small basket of either flower, or both
2 egg whites
Caster sugar as needed
A small flat-shaped paint brush
A tweezers
A wire rack for drying the flowers

Discard any flowers that are bruised or misshapen. Take each flower and remove all the stem and any green material at the base. Make sure the flowers are completely dry. Beat the egg white until frothy. Set up a production line. Flowers, egg white and sugar.

Grip the base of each flower and 'paint' each flower on both sides with the frothy egg white. Dip the brush into the caster sugar and paint each flower, making sure the surface of the flower is fully coated with sugar. You may use a sugar shaker or a teaspoon to sugar any part of the flower that has been missed in the dipping process.

Carefully place each flower base-side downwards on the wire rack. Dry in a warm place. If the air is high in humidity, place them in an oven set to the lowest possible temperature with the oven door slightly open. Store the dried flowers, interleaved with tissue paper or waxed paper, in a box or wide-necked jar. Store in a dark dry place.

You may wish to keep small children away as they are so delicious they eat them as fast as you make them.

GORSE SYRUP

500g gorse flowers

A few tablespoons of fresh lemon juice, or to taste

1 litre water

500g sugar

Boil the flowers and water together for 10 minutes. Strain through a jelly bag. Place sugar and strained juice in a pot and cook slowly, stirring, until sugar is dissolved. Then boil for about five minutes, skimming any froth from the surface. Cool before bottling in small sterilised bottles. Best stored in a fridge.

Wild Strawberry

*Fragaria vescca * Irish sú talún fiáin*

Wild strawberries grow naturally all over the northern hemisphere and they thrive and fruit generously all summer long.

Cultivated strawberries were bred from two wild varieties, one from Eastern America the other from an area that runs from Alaska to Patagonia. Native European wood and alpine strawberries are a perennial with a long fruiting season. The berries are small. The leaves are pure bright-green and matt as opposed to the shiny, larger and darker leaves of cultivated strawberries.

Archaeological evidence suggests our ancestors have been eating wild strawberries since the Stone Age. Cultivation began in ancient Persia and spread to Europe where they were cultivated until a few hundred years ago when the larger, garden strawberry gradually became established. Only in France and Turkey is the extra effort of harvesting deemed worth it for the superior flavour and aroma.

WHERE TO LOOK

Laneways, road verges, banks, grassland, hillsides, gravel paths, woodland edges and clearings. It's happy in partial shade and grows anywhere as long as it is not extremely dry or wet. An

evergreen plant which makes it easy to spot your gathering place in winter.

WHAT IT LOOKS LIKE

Multi-stemmed with a three-leaf arrangement. Wild berries and leaves are smaller than cultivated, a pure, bright green in colour and softer in texture than the garden variety's larger, darker green leaves with a sheen. Both carry white flowers and propagate by runners that shoot out from the parent plant and quickly grow into new ones.

HOW TO PICK

Choose a place away from traffic fumes. Bring with you a flat basket and patience: the berries being small take time to gather. I wear garden knee-pads so I can get close down and see behind the leaves where fruits lurk. Small fingers and young eyes work best, but the berries

rarely reach the basket! Ripe berries are red and come away easily from the hull saving you work at home. The leaves picked while the plant is in blossom make the best flavoured 'tea'.

HOW TO PREPARE

Remove any green hulls and check for the occasional insect. They are unlikely to need washing. Eat or preserve as soon as possible. If you only have a few you can freeze them on trays for short periods.

TRADITIONAL USES

The most common use is to eat them fresh with cream. Other uses include preserving in sugar syrup for use as a dessert sauce, or to flavour ice cream, in gourmet jam, to make liqueurs or cordials, to flavour fruit fools, and for fruit tarts, cakes and muffins. The leaves, fresh or dried, make a delicious herbal 'tea'. The berries were once used to clean teeth and ease the inflammation of facial spots and pimples.

PRESERVING WILD STRAWBERRIES

The two main methods are in sugar syrup and in alcohol.

To preserve wild strawberries in sugar syrup follow the methods described in the Preserving section, using a medium-strength sugar syrup and packing the berries closely in the jar. A variation is to add a little white wine in place of some of the water.

Wild Strawberry, Bilberry, Blackberry and Rose Water Jelly.

WILD STRAWBERRY, BILBERRY, BLACKBERRY AND ROSE WATER JELLY

WHAT GOES IN

1 handful wild strawberries

2 handfuls wild bilberries

2 handfuls wild blackberries

750ml water

400g organic sugar

½ vanilla pod

5 leaves of gelatine

4–5 drops of rose water

250ml organic sparkling white wine

HOW IT GOES

Place the water and sugar into a saucepan with the half vanilla pod, split. Bring slowly to boil to dissolve the sugar. Soak the gelatine leaves in a bowl of cold of water. Add gelatine into hot liquid and stir until you are sure gelatine is fully dissolved through the liquid. Whisk rose water drops into the liquid and add the white wine.

Use a large mould, just as your grandmother did, for placing in the centre of the table. Or, use individual dariole moulds or coffee cups or whatever shape you like. Place a layer of the wild strawberries in the bottom of mould and just cover with the jelly liquid. Allow this layer to set in fridge. Keep the remainder of the liquid jelly warm. When set, add another layer of berries. This time using all three types of berries (wild strawberries, wild bilberries and wild blackberries). Repeat layering process until mould is full.

HOW TO FINISH

Allow to set in fridge. To turn out, dip jelly mould into hot water for a few seconds and turn out onto serving dish.

WHAT YOU GET

Is an adult jelly of summer fruits that will transport you back! This jelly pays homage to the illusive and hard to harvest wild strawberry. That's why it has pride of place for the first spoon at the top of the mould when it is inverted. We feel that the rose water adds to the deep perfume taste of this fabulous wild fruit.

WILD STRAWBERRY IN SCHNAPPS OR VODKA

1 bottle schnaps or vodka
Sugar, to taste

Prick each prepared berry a few times with a needle or cocktail stick, and place in a Kilner-type jar. Fill to the halfway mark. Pour in sugar and shake to about the same level. Top up with your chosen spirit, which should be at least 40% proof. Cover. Store in a cool, dark place. Shake every few days until the sugar is dissolved. Whole berries are best consumed within three months. The liquid, strained through a jellly bag makes a delicious flavoured liqueur. It will keep for quite a while longer in sterlised bottles.

Wild Chanterelle

Cantharellus cibarius * Irish *beacán buí fiáin*

The chanterelle is a fairly common mushroom. It is extremely pretty and its bright colour makes it easy to spot in woodlands. It is beloved all over Europe and frequently gathered and sold at markets.

WHERE TO LOOK

The chanterelle is found in all kinds of woodland and particularly favours birch, beech and coniferous forests with mossy ground. It is in season from July until the first frosts. It tends to grow in clusters.

WHAT IT LOOKS LIKE

The colour is a bright and deep yellow rather like the egg yolk from a free-range hen. It is uniform in colour (unlike the false chanterelle which has an orange colour that is graded to a darker centre). It is cup- or funnel-shaped with an upturned cap. Underneath it has gill-shaped ridges that run down to the tapered stem. The aroma tends to vary from a fruity apricot to spicy and earthier.

Although rare in Ireland, it has been known for people to confuse chanterelle with the poisonous *Cortinarius speciosissimus*. The colour of chanterelle is bright yellow rather than pale ochre to orange. The stem of chanterelle tapers towards the end rather than being thickened at the base. The 3-10 cm cap has a flattened incurved margin when young. This becomes wavy, lobed and depressed in the centre as it matures rather than being convex in shape. The gills are egg-yellow, narrow, forked and fusing into one another rather than being like true gills. The chanterelle yellow flesh smells faintly of apricots rather than of radish. If you do a spore test by leaving the mushroom face down on white paper for several hours, the spores of the edible chanterelle are almost white; the poisonous *Cortinarius speciosissimus* has rust-coloured spores.

Note: If in doubt, do not eat. Take a picture and show it to an expert.

HOW TO PICK

Use a small knife and cut off close to the ground. They are tender so lay them carefully in a flat basket.

HOW TO PREPARE

Wipe with damp kitchen paper to remove any earth. They will keep quite fresh for a few days in the fridge.

TRADITIONAL USES

Wild chanterelle have an affinity to eggs, potatoes, butter and cream. The flavour compounds are fat soluble and alcohol soluble making them suitable to cook in butter, oil, cream, wine and other alcohol. The most common uses are in sauces, in egg, potato and bacon dishes, soups, and as a flavouring ingredient in stews and slow-cooked dishes.

PRESERVING WILD CHANTERELLE

Chanterelles are most suited to being preserved in oil or dried. They dry so successfully that many gourmets hold that the flavour is intensified by drying. The dried chanterelle is also ground into a powder to use as a seasoning.

Preserving in oil is well suited to all mushrooms.

Pickling tends to mask the distinctive flavour of chanterelles. It would not be my first choice, although it is popular in Asian food cultures, either alone or with a variety of fungi.

Make sure mushrooms for preservation are blemish free and not too old. Whichever method you decide to choose follow the methods in the Preservation section.

WILD CHANTERELLE GOULASH

WHAT GOES IN

1kg wild chanterelles

2 organic onions, finely diced

2 organic red peppers, diced

100g organic streaky bacon or pancetta, diced

1 organic garlic clove, finely chopped

2 tbsp organic tomato purée

1 rounded tbsp sweet paprika powder

300ml organic vegetable or chicken stock

Wild Chanterelle Goulash.

A splash of organic white wine vinegar

50ml organic cream

½ bunch parsley, chopped

Organic crème fraiche

Sea salt and black pepper

Organic rapeseed oil for frying

HOW IT GOES

Brush or wash the chanterelles very quickly under running water, pat dry.

Heat some oil in a pan and fry the mushrooms quickly, put in a sieve set over a bowl and save the poured-off liquid.

Fry the diced onions over medium heat until golden, add the peppers, garlic and bacon and fry for another 5 minutes. Reduce the heat, put the tomato purée in and stir well, avoid burning the purée. Add the paprika powder and then deglaze it with the vinegar.

Pour the stock and the saved liquid from frying the chanterelles and cook it gently for 15–20 minutes. Add the cream, season with salt and pepper and blitz in a processor.

Strain through a sieve into a pot. Put the chanterelles back in the sauce and cook for a few more minutes.

HOW TO FINISH

Fold in the chopped parsley and season to taste. Garnish with, or fold in, a dollop of crème fraiche

WHAT YOU GET

Is a summer-special goulash with all the flavour of the chanterelle.

Perfect served as its original decreed, with bread dumplings, or maybe with pasta or rice instead. As a supper with friends or even a TV snack. Just spoon over a slice of fresh grilled bread, and enjoy.

CHANTERELLE WITH BACON, ONIONS AND WINE

A brilliant way of making a small amount of chanterelles go a long way.

500g fresh chanterelles, sliced if large
110g smoked, streaky bacon, diced into small cubes
A large knob of butter
1 small onion
1 glass white wine
A handful of fresh parsley, finely chopped

Trim and wipe the chanterelles with a damp cloth. Cook the bacon in the butter in a pan until the fat runs. Add the onion and cook gently for a minute or two. Add the parsley and wine and season to taste with pepper and salt. Raise the heat and bubble for a few minutes. Next reduce the heat to very low (or pop in a cool oven) and continue to cook very gently for about fifteen minutes. Check that it does not become too dry and shake the pan so that it does not stick. Serve with good bread.

Wild Bilberry

Vaccinium myrtillus * Irish *fraochán*

Wild bilberries are often called fraughans, whorts or wild blueberries. They are the first wild berry to ripen. This is a cause for celebration with Fraughan Sunday, the last Sunday in July, being a survival of the pre-Christian Celtic festival of Lughnasa. Young people gathered berries in the hills and girls baked the berries into a cake which they presented to a chosen 'fella' at a dance in the evening.

The fruit can be eaten raw or cooked and incorporated into a variety of tarts, desserts, preserves and drinks, and used to flavour spirits. They are most often preserved by drying, or with sugar.

WHERE TO LOOK

Found on hillsides and mountain slopes (particularly where heather and ferns grow), heathland and acid woodland from sea level to over 1,000 metres.

WHAT IT LOOKS LIKE

A low-growing plant from 25–60cm tall. It has a creeping rhizome that allows spreading. Where you find one plant there are likely to be others. A long line stretching along a roadside or walking track is quite usual. From the rhizome erect stems rise with small, very slightly toothed, pale green leaves when young. On high ground or windy locations they turn dark green and acquire a rusty look on top. Other wild plants and flowers often obscure them.

HOW TO PICK

Choose a place away from traffic fumes and wait until they are fully ripe; this time will vary depending on height, aspect and light levels. The berries go from green, to red, to black with a bluish bloom when ripe. They grow singly and are often hidden under the leaves and on the young leaf growth near the base of the plant. The plant may look empty of berries. Move aside the leaves to pick, looking methodically, from to back to front and top to bottom, and you will find berries unless someone has been there before you. You might like to wear thin gloves to avoid staining your fingers and nail beds purple. In truth, children's small fingers are better suited to the task and if you have a bad back bring a garden kneeler.

HOW TO PREPARE

Remove stray leaves and any badly bruised berries. If you wish, give them a quick rinse and dry on kitchen paper. They may be eaten fresh or preserved for later use.

TRADITIONAL USES

The most traditional use of all is to use them dried as 'hedgerow currants' in 'curranty' soda bread or scones. But, of course, they have many uses: in jams and jellies, either alone or with apples, in the Fraughan Sunday sponge cakes, in tarts, steamed suet puddings, pancakes, muffins, muesli, granola, fruit fool, fruit soufflé, syrup, cordial, wine, to flavour and add a vibrant colour to festive sprits like gin, vodka and *poitín*, in ice-cream or sorbets, or in a mixed jar of hedgerow Rumtopf. They could also be used as a fruit soup, or bottled and used as compote with ice cream or plain puddings.

PRESERVING WILD BILBERRIES

By Drying

Spread out on trays and dry in an ultra-slow oven, or on a tray in a dry, airy, sunny place indoors. They do attract insects so you may wish to cover with muslin.

See also bottling, making liqueur, wine and vinegar in the Preservation section. For preserving with sugar see recipe on p161.

WILD BILBERRY
CHEESECAKE MUFFINS

WHAT GOES IN

Muffin mix:

225ml organic milk

75g cold unsalted organic butter, cut into chunks

2 organic eggs

225g organic plain flour

125g organic sugar

2 tsp baking powder

Pinch of sea salt

100g fresh wild bilberries, washed

Cheesecake mix:

150g organic soft cream cheese

160g organic sugar

1 organic egg

Vanilla seeds and pulp from ½ vanilla pod

HOW IT GOES

Pop paper muffin cases into 12-cup muffin tin.

For the cheesecake mixture, combine the cheese, sugar, egg

and vanilla pulp and set aside.

For the muffins, put the milk and butter in a small pot and heat slightly, stir until the butter is melted. Take off the heat and let cool down, then beat in the eggs. In a bowl, mix the flour, sugar, salt and baking powder together, pour in the milk-butter mix and work it until well combined. Gently fold the berries into the mixture.

Spoon the muffin mix into the prepared muffin cases and top this up with 2 tsp of the cheesecake mix. Then with a metal skewer or thin knife, swirl this mixture right to the base of the paper cases.

Bake the muffins for about 20 minutes between 180°C and 200°C. Allow them cool for 10 minutes in the tin before taking them out.

WHAT YOU GET

A lighter muffin with the cheesecake that really suits the fresh summer taste of wild bilberries. If you can resist them straight out of the oven, re-warm before serving with some good strong coffee, perfect.

Wild Bilberry Cheesecake Muffins.

WILD BILBERRY
AND ALMOND DESSERT

500g sugar-syruped wild bilberries
or 125g dried wild bilberries
100g sugar
Zest of orange
1 tbsp sherry

Cake mix:
250g ground almonds
Zest of large orange
175g caster sugar
4 medium eggs
Pinch of salt

If using dried berries, reconstitute them by soaking for 30 minutes in sugar syrup. If using berries preserved in sugar syrup, reduce the amount of sugar in this recipe by half.

Place berries, sugar, zest and sherry into a warm oven for 15 minutes. Remove and stir to dissolve sugar. Meanwhile, make the cake mix. Beat eggs yolks and sugar till fluffy. In a separate bowl beat egg whites to stiff peaks (add a pinch of salt). Combine egg yolks and ground almonds and zest until just mixed. Gently fold in egg whites and combine. Pour two-thirds of the berries and syrup into an ovenproof dish. Top with cake mix and bake for 15 minutes until an inserted skewer comes out clean. Serve warm or cold with remainder of berries and whipped cream.

WILD BILBERRIES IN SUGAR SYRUP

500g wild bilberries, cleaned
125g sugar
125ml water

Place water and sugar in a pot and eat gently, stirring until the sugar is dissolved. Boil for 2 minutes.

Pack the berries tightly into sterilised jars, filling the jars a third at a time and adding the sugar syrup to the same level as you go.

Cover and place jars on a rack or folded tea towel in the bottom of the pot, choosing a pot deep enough for the water to cover the jars by 3cm. Pour hot water over the jar and bring to the boil. Cook for about 15 minutes. Remove from the pot and place on a wooden board or tea towel to cool. Wait for 24 hours and test the seal.

The lids of screw top jars should have pulled down into slightly concave position as they cool. This indicates you have a good seal. If the lid pops up when pressed the seal is not good.

To test the seal on glass jars with a rubber seals and a clamp, turn upside down so that the fruit is pressed against the top. If any bubbles appear the seal is not good. It is possible to re-process; otherwise use as soon as possible. Stored in a cool, dark place the preserve will keep for up to a year.

Wild Field Mushroom

Agaricus campestris * Irish *beacán coiteann fiáin*

The wild field mushroom is the most commonly collected mushroom. Ireland is a land with a vast amount of pasture that until relatively recent times was not 'improved' with chemical fertilizers. When meadows were almost carpeted with white-coloured field mushrooms everyone knew what they looked like. Although not as plentiful as they once were, they can still be found all over the countryside. Field mushrooms are tasty and versatile, can be eaten fresh, raw or cooked, or preserved by drying, pickling in oil, or made into a traditional condiment – mushroom ketchup.

WHERE TO LOOK

Grassland and meadows (particularly permanent pasture land) rather than land that is used in crop rotation. They are more plentiful on good land, especially land that has been fertilized by cattle, sheep and horses. However, you may also find them on golf courses in 'the rough' or on the lazy acre (meadow on road verges), on cultivated land where there are grassy field edges or turning circles for combine harvesters, on set-aside land, sometimes even on the grassy banks of new roads, and on sports grounds that are used in summer. They tend to favour dense clumps of grass, making them difficult to see.

WHAT IT LOOKS LIKE

A field mushroom varies in size from the usual 4–10cm across to the, admittedly rare, 60cm. It has a white, turning to cream-coloured cap. The stem tapers towards the base and has a delicate ring or apron. The gills start out pale pink; as they mature they turn slightly reddish and then, as they mature even more, and the 'button opens', the gills turn brown. The aroma is of fresh mushroom.

HOW TO PICK

Carry a basket (or a half-opened umbrella) so that they don't get crushed. Walk your potential grassland systematically, keeping your eyes down, scanning the grass a few feet in front of you – this helps prevent trampling a good mushroom. Cut with a small knife. If the gills are pure white, or the base stains yellow, or there are wart-like bumps on the surface, discard it! It is not a field mushroom.

HOW TO PREPARE

Cut off the earthy base and wipe with a damp clean cloth. Do not peel or you will lose the flavour. They may be eaten fresh, or preserved.

TRADITIONAL USES

Field mushrooms have long been a traditional breakfast food – either as part of the 'full Irish', or on their own cooked in bacon fat. They were cooked used in soups, stews, tarts and salads.

Renowned food historian Dorothy Hartley recorded that 'small button mushrooms are best for pickling and cooking in milk; rounder pink-gilled ones can be cooked and preserved in a variety of ways, fully opened reddish-gilled flats are best grilled with butter; when they become darker underneath but still dry, they are good for drying and flavouring, and when gone quite black are only good for ketchup'.

Mushrooms were preserved in much the same ways as today and most recipes and methods of preservation are interchangeable.

PRESERVING WILD FIELD MUSHROOMS

They may be made into a ketchup or relish They may also be dried, a method is described in the section on Preservation. Another interesting way involved lightly cooking and immersing in combination of oil, lemons juice and vinegar.

For 1kg of field mushrooms take the juice of two lemons, 3–4 cloves garlic, a few bay leaves, peppercorns, 100ml wine vinegar and 60ml rapeseed or olive oil and water, and simmer boil for fifteen minutes. Cut mushrooms into quarters (or even eighths if very large) and place in a pot and add more boiling water if needed to bring liquid level with the mushrooms. Simmer for five minutes and allow to cool in the liquid. Drain. Place in sterilised jars and cover with oil and a well-fitting cap. Add additional spices or herbs as you wish. Store in a cool, dry place.

Wild Field Mushroom Duxelle.

WILD FIELD MUSHROOM DUXELLE

WHAT GOES IN

500g wild field mushrooms
Juice of an organic lemon
4 tbsp dry sherry
3 organic shallots, finely minced
2 tbsp organic rapeseed oil
4 tbsp clarified organic butter
Sea salt and organic black pepper

HOW IT GOES

Clean the wild field mushrooms to remove any dirt. Finely dice or mince the mushrooms. You can blitz in a processor; however your aim is to have very small, separate pieces, not a mash.

In a wide-based pan, heat the oil, add the shallots and sweat over a gentle heat until soft. Add mushrooms, lemon juice, sherry; season. Reduce the heat and cook slowly for up to 40 minutes, stirring occasionally or until the mushroom mix has reduced to a firm, slightly moist consistency. Taste and season to taste.

HOW TO FINISH

Use straight away or spoon into sterilised Kilner jars. Let cool and pour warmed clarified butter over to seal before putting the lid on. Stored in a fridge it will keep for a couple of weeks.

WHAT YOU GET

This works really well with pastry and beef, Wellington style. However, you cannot beat it as a stuffing for a roast Sunday chicken, or salmon or trout. Moistened up slightly with cream, seasoning and a dribble of dry sherry it works really well as ravioli filler.

MUSHROOM RELISH

This traditional Irish mushroom ketchup, unlike thick, glumpy tomato ketchup, is a thin, intensely flavoured, lightly spiced condiment. It can be used to add zest to a huge variety of soups, stews, and sauces, or simply when it takes your fancy. Collected by Florence Irwin, the 'cookin' woman' who taught cooking skills in rural County Down in Northern Ireland. Her real passion was collecting and trying out the traditional recipes and ways within rural areas. She wrote regular articles about her discoveries in *The Northern Whig* and later they were collected into two books.

Choose a cool place (the dairy was traditional). As the mushroom season progresses, mushrooms are placed in an earthenware jar as they are gathered and each layer covered in salt. Each time you gather some more, add another layer and sprinkle salt on top and press down well. Continue until you have a thick black liquid. Pour this liquid into small sterilised bottles with tightly-fitting caps or corks. Other flavourings of your choice may be added at this stage. The most usual in Irish food culture was pepper and onion.

Wild Blackberry

Rubus fruticosus *Irish *sméar dubh*

The botanical name of this native plant is *Rubus fruticosus,* but it is variously called a briar, or bramble, and the edible fruit is simply known as a blackberry.

A multi-use plant: ripe fruit is eaten for pleasure, leaves are used as a dressing on wounds, the roots for an orange dye, the berries to dye hair black. The tangled thorns caught sheep wool (and so provided spinning for the landless poor) and Celtic peoples used the briar to ward off evil spirits. The folk belief that the *púca* spat (or worse) on the berry at Hallowe'en prevented folk eating berries that were grey-mildewed.

WHERE TO LOOK

You see it in field and road banks, hedgerows and woods, from sea level up to 350m.

WHAT IT LOOKS LIKE

Brambles, up to 1½ metres high, grow in a tangle of arching branches that root from the tips. Along the branch are sharp thorns and groups of 3-5 toothed leaves, mid- to dark-green. The buds are greyish-green and open into white or pale pink flowers which bloom from May to autumn. The fruit is a collection of small one-seeded drupes which start out pale green, turn red and ripen to a purplish-black. They are rich in vitamin C.

HOW TO PICK

You need a walking-stick to bring down the best berries at the top of the bush; wear thorn-proof or very old clothes. It is hard to pick the berries with gloves on, but not to wear them results in the area under your nails being dyed black for days. Bring a bar of soap with you and draw your nails through soap until the area is packed full, renew at regular intervals. Plastic bags get ripped to shreds. An old-fashioned billy-can with a metal handle is ideal, but anything small and deep works.

Best picked after a few dry days. Ripe berries come away easily from the hull. Pick the largest, fully ripe berries only. Ignore green or red berries and any with mildew. A traditional council of perfection is to first pick the lowest berry on each cluster (which ripens first) and place into a separate container – these are the largest, sweetest and finest berries and should be eaten raw, being soft and full of juice. Later in the season the secondary berries ripen; less juicy but good for jams and puddings.

HOW TO PREPARE

Discard hulls and leaves. Place fruit in a colander and rinse with gently running water. Spread on kitchen paper to remove excess water. Use as soon as is practical.

TRADITIONAL USES

Jam, jelly, fruit butters and cheeses, a filling for tarts, fruit crumble, sponge pudding, fruit compotes, as a fruit flavour in porridge, and made into a cordial, a syrup, and wine. More recently used to flavour vinegar, alcohol, sorbets and ice cream. The leaves may be dried and used as a herb tea.

PRESERVING WILD BLACKBERRIES

The berries may be preserved as jam, jelly, fruit butter, fruit cheese, chutney, and flavoured vinegar. The strained juice can be mixed with honey and cider as a cordial, or fermented into wine. Follow the methods in the Preservation section.

WILD BLACKBERRY WINE VINEGAR

WHAT GOES IN

1kg wild blackberries
750ml organic white wine
250ml white balsamic vinegar

HOW IT GOES

Sterilise a suitable wide-necked container for 5 minutes with boiling water, pour off.

Wash the wild blackberries, let excess water drip off and place the berries into the container. Although there will be a natural yeast on the berries, it is best to use the small amount of vinegar as a starting agent.

Slightly warm up the wine and the vinegar, pour over the berries, seal the container with clean muslin. This will allow air to interact with the natural yeasts and vinegar. Leave in a warm dark location to ferment. Stir daily to ensure that all the fermenting yeasts are well mixed through the liquid. This can take up to 2 or 3 weeks.

However, after a few days you will start to notice that vinegary scent. The intensity of this and your requirement for what you would like to achieve, will decide as to when you finish the process.

HOW TO FINISH

Now you can strain the blackberry wine vinegar mix overnight through a muslin cloth into another sterilised container and the next day seal off in sterilised bottles for future use. Also for future use, set aside a small amount to use as a staring agent for next year's crop!

WHAT YOU GET

Blackberry wine vinegar adds a super dimension to vinaigrettes and other salad dressings. It will also make for interesting mustards, mayonnaise and even ketchups. Works really well in chutneys, pickles and relishes. Also as a simple, but fruitier, alternative to lemon juice in any recipe. However, as a gift to your friends it works best.

BLACKBERRY AND CARRAGEEN PUDDING

15g dried carrageen
900ml milk
Rind of half a lemon
Sugar to taste
250g blackberries, or a jar of blackberries preserved in syrup, or 100ml blackberry dessert sauce, or melted blackberry and crab apple jelly

Rehydrate the carrageen and rinse in cold water. Place in a pot with the milk and lemon rind. Slowly bring to boiling point. Sweeten to taste. Strain to remove the carrageen and half-fill small bowls, glasses, or ramekins with the liquid. Place in a cool fridge to set.

If using fresh blackberries pick over, removing any that are damaged and all leaves and twigs. Rinse briefly under cold running water. Place in a pot with sugar to taste; cook briefly and sweeten to taste. If there is a lot of juice, remove berries and boil the juice until reduced and slightly syrupy.

To serve, spoon the blackberries with the thickened juice, or the blackberries preserved in syrup, or the melted blackberry jelly, over the carrageen blancmange and allow to set again in a cool place.

BLACKBERRY SORBET

375ml water
225g sugar
375ml blackberry juice

Place water in a pot; add the sugar and stir until dissolved. Bring to the boil and cook until you have a syrupy texture. Cool. Mix the syrup and blackberry juice and place in the freezer. Take care not to freeze it for too long before serving as the sorbet should be quite soft in texture. Serve in glasses.

Wild Rowanberry

Sorbus aucuparia * Irish *caorthann*

The wild rowanberry is a native tree throughout Ireland and is more often called the mountain ash, a name that gives a clue to where you are most likely to find these trees growing in the wild. On account of its beautiful spring blossoms and plentiful red berries in autumn, it has become a popular garden tree in the suburbs, in town-planting schemes, and along motorway embankments – areas that tend to be polluted. It is wiser to seek them out in their natural habitat.

WHERE TO LOOK

Rowans will grow pretty well anywhere, but in their natural, self-seeded state they thrive on mountains, hills, rocky land, particularly when the soil (such as it is) tends to be peaty and a tad acid rather than chalk or alkaline. You will also find them near old houses and cottages as it was traditional to plant one near a house.

WHAT IT LOOKS LIKE

Rowan trees are relatively small with a smooth silvery-grey bark. They are lightly branched, with leaves that are all the same size, pointed, with serrated edges and arranged in about six opposite pairs along the stalk. The flowers bloom in late April, early May. The blossom is white and has a faint almond scent. The berries grow in clusters and, depending how good the summer is, turn from a pale colour through orange and then to red from August to October.

HOW TO PICK

Do not choose a place where you know people feed birds and where there are a lot of blackbirds and thrushes. These birds will often eat the berries before they are truly ripe for preservation and culinary use. Bring a basket, a walking stick, or a crutch to pull the branches down, and gather whole clusters.

HOW TO PREPARE

Remove leaves and all the stalks. Wash berries with cold water.

TRADITIONAL USES

The Celtic druids held it to be a sacred tree capable of warding off evil spirits. In the telling of the sagas as recorded in early medieval times eating just three rowanberries had the power to reverse the aging process by more than two-thirds. All the Celtic peoples turned the berries into alcohol: the ancient Irish into wine and to flavour mead; the Scots into spirits; the Welsh brewed it in a variety of ways to make ale, and a cider or perry-style brew. The fruit is sour and has a unique flavour. It makes an interesting wine, a wonderful jelly, and a tasty jam mixed with crab apples or blackberries. Rowanberry jelly is served with game, feathered and furred, particularly venison and used to add flavour to sauces for game or even a simple jus or gravy. It is used as a delicious filling for sponge cakes, a glaze for fruit tea breads like barm brack, melted and poured over a red berry or stone fruit tart and allowed to set.

Raw rowanberries are very astringent and are not pleasant to eat. The seeds contain parasorbic acid, which may cause indigestion.

PRESERVING WILD ROWANBERRIES

. . . .

The most usual method is to cook ripe berries until they are soft, strain and use the juice either with crab apples to make a traditional jelly, or added with other berries and fruit in mixed hedgerow jams or syrups. It may be fermented with sugar and yeast to make wine. Methods may be found in the Preservation section.

WILD ROWANBERRY SCHNAPPS

WHAT GOES IN

One-eight fill bottle or demi-john
with granulated sugar
Top to the same mark with dry
sherry
Fill to the threequarter line with wild rowanberries
Fill to the top with vodka

HOW IT GOES

Remove stems. Wash, dry and freeze for 24 hours. Rowans contain sorbic, bitter and tannic acids, freezing will mellow or dissipate these. After defrosting, lay in one layer on a baking tray and lightly press with a potato masher to ever so lightly burst the fruits, before adding to the bottle. As schnapps it should be fairly-dry, so the amount of sugar is personal. The sherry works a treat and adds super depth.

HOW TO FINISH

Shake every third day for three weeks, then shake every week for three weeks. Leave to settle and strain after a further three weeks.

WHAT YOU GET

Is a super-dry traditional and refreshing fruit schnapps; if you prefer a sweeter more liqueur-style to share after dinner or as a pressie for your family or friends, simply add more sugar to the recipe.

What you also get is a schnapps oozing with all the flavours of those fabulous strained fruits, having been fully 'cooked' in the vodka, sherry and sugars.

Use these fruits as a pulp to add to stuffing for late summer game like wild rabbit and grain-harvesting woodpigeon, or simply as an ingredient in breads, cakes, sauces and desserts.

WILD ROWANBERRY JELLY

4kg wild rowanberries, washed and stalks removed
2kg crab apples (or cooking apples), washed but not peeled
3 litres water
Sugar, warmed (amount calculated when you measure juice)

Place rowanberries, apples and water in a large preserving pot. Bring to the boil. Boil gently for about 40 minutes. Strain the contents of the pot through a jelly bag or pillowcase, leaving it to drip overnight. Do not squeeze or the jelly will become cloudy. Measure the juice and calculate 500g sugar for each ½kg of juice. Boil for about ten minutes and add the warmed sugar; boil again for ten minutes. Skim off any scum that rises to the top. Boil until setting temperature is reached, or test for a setting point in the usual way. Pour into sterilised jars and seal at once with the caps.

Note: You may add spices – your choice. However, plain jelly is more versatile.

WILD ROWANBERRY LEMONADE

1kg wild rowanberries
1kg rhubarb
1kg crab apple
1 tbsp citric acid
1 litre water
300g sugar per litre of juice

Crush the rowanberries and place in a bowl with sliced rhubarb and apple. Sprinkle the citric acid over the mixture. Pour over boiling water and stir. Cover and leave in a cool place for 2 days, stirring it at frequent intervals. Strain off the juice, add the sugar and stir until dissolved. Pour into sterilised bottles. Serve 50/50 with ice-cold water or soda water

WILD ROWANBERRY AND APPLE JAM

1kg wild rowanberries, prepared
1kg cooking apples, peeled, cored and sliced
3kg sugar, warmed
A little water

Cook the apples in a tiny bit of water until soft and then process through a food mill or strain. Place berries with a little water and boil for about 10 minutes. Process these through a food mill or strain. Place berry and apple purée in a pot with the warmed sugar. Stir over the heat until the sugar is dissolved; then boil until setting point is reached. Pot into sterilised jars and cover. Store in a cool dry place.

Wild Damson

Prunus domestica *Irish *daimsín fiáin*

The whole business of what's a damson, what's a plum, what's a bullace is fraught with confusion and different schools of thought. To some, bullace is one of a number of wild and feral varieties of plum. Damsons are thought to have developed from bullace and the plum is a domesticated damson. All appear to have a connection to the wild cherry. All are stone fruit and the flesh of the juicy, plum-shaped fruits range in colour from yellow, to red, to a dark, blackish purple. The Irish keep it simple: what looks like a wild damson is called *daimsín fiáin*.

WHERE TO LOOK

Whether native, introduced, or feral, they appear to sow themselves without too much trouble and given a bit of shelter in a hedgerow, or corner of a field, or a country garden gone wild, they are there for the picking of their delicious and versatile fruit. The fruits do have rather a tart flavour and the skin can be acidic.

WHAT IT LOOKS LIKE

It is a tree, rather than a bush like sloe. The leaves are oval ending in a pointed top. The branches of bullace/damson are sometimes

spiny, while those of feral plum are smooth. The fruits (in a range of colours) are 5–12cm long. The flesh of bullace sticks to the stone, the others (when ripe) separate cleanly from the stone.

HOW TO PICK

When the fruit is ripe and juicy and beginning to fall to the ground naturally, they are ready to pick. No special equipment is needed – a stick to draw down high branches, a basket for the fruit. If they are very ripe you could spread a large piece of material around the tree and give it a gentle shake.

HOW TO PREPARE

Remove any leaves and stalks. A quick wash and they are ready to use, either fresh or preserved.

TRADITIONAL USES

Traditionally eaten fresh (with sugar to sweeten) in tarts, puddings, cakes and fruity desserts. Bottling whole was common. A curious method mentioned by Mrs Beaton was to place them in jars, cover with boiling water and then top with a thick layer of mutton fat. In Asia a traditional preserve is plum sauce to eat with crispy duck. The fruits may be puréed and dried into a fruit leather which can be diced and added as a dried ingredient for cakes, fruit porridge, or muesli.

PRESERVING WILD DAMSONS

Preserved with sugar, the fruits may be made into jams, fruit butters and sauces and a rich chutney or spicy relish. The strained juice may be made into jelly. In Eastern and Northern Europe the fruits are distilled into Slivovitz, a brandy-type spirit. In countries where home-distilling is illegal they are added as a flavouring to brandy, vodka or gin. Details of these methods are to be found in the section on Preservation.

WILD DAMSON
SWEETMEAT OR CHEESE

WHAT GOES IN

2kg wild damsons

1kg organic sugar

100g cornflour

25g icing sugar

500ml water

HOW IT GOES

Simmer the wild damsons gently in water until soft and mushy. Pass through a sieve to obtain the wet pulp.

Measure pulp, add an equal quantity of sugar. Heat in a pot and stir constantly to dissolve sugar. Bring up to a high heat, stir to reduce until you have a thick purée. When mix is very thick it will come away from the side of the pan and is at setting point. Pour into shallow parchment-lined tin to set.

HOW TO FINISH

Allow to chill and set. Mix the cornflour with the icing sugar to make a dusting powder. Cut the damson cheese into small squares and coat with the dusting powder. Store in an airtight container.

WHAT YOU GET

Is an old-fashioned fruit cheese or sweet-meat. Our grand-mothers would have told us that, with the high sugar content,

WILD DAMSON

this would keep forever. No doubt, these days it is required by some EU Committee to have a 'Use by Date'... you decide!

What you also get is a great wild alternative to traditional membrillo, and works just as well as an accompaniment for a cheeseboard or just as an energy booster on winter foraging trips. Alternatively, the damson cheese could also be used for baking with breads and cake recipes.

SAVOURY WILD DAMSON OR WILD PLUM SAUCE

500g wild damsons or wild plums
275ml dry white wine
1 tbsp wine vinegar
2 tbsp honey
Sugar to taste

Place fruit, wine and vinegar in a pot and simmer gently until the fruit is soft. Sieve to remove the stones. Return to the pan, add the honey and sugar to taste, and reduce until you have about 250ml of sauce or it is pleasingly thickened.

It is easy to convert this into Asian-style by the addition of spices.

BOTTLED WHOLE DAMSON OR PLUMS

Wash the fruit and remove the stalks but not the stones. Place the fruit in wide-necked glass jars. Cover with tightly-fitting cling film. (Mrs Beaton used a bladder!) In a large, deep pot spread a clean tea towel on the base and then place the jars in the pot. Pour in cold water close to the neck of the jars. Bring the water slowly to boiling point, then turn off the heat. The jars should remain in the pot until the contents are fully cold. Remove the cling film. The fruit will have shrunk a little. Spoon sugar right up to the neck of the jars. Cover with tightly-fitting lids. (Mrs Beaton suggests corks and wax.) Store in a cool, dark place.

Wild Cep, Penny Bun

Boletus edulis * Irish *borróg pingine*

Dubbed the king of wild mushrooms, the cep is a member of the *Boletus* family of fungi, the most obvious feature of which is that in place of the gills there are sponge-like tubes on the underside of the cap. The *Boletus* family of mushrooms are highly identifiable. They are prized in France, where they are called ceps, Italy where they carry the curious name *porcini* – piglets! Here, and in Britain, the common name is The Penny Bun on account of the round cap. There are a number of other fungi that belong to the *Boletus* family, but here we concentrate on *Boletus edulis*.

WHERE TO LOOK

Commonly found in mixed woodlands, all the *Boletus* family of mushrooms are mycorrhizal, that is they grow with particular species of host trees. Fortunately, these trees are very common trees in Ireland, so they are there for the picking right through from late summer until November. Early ceps are shy and seem to like light-speckled woodlands. Ceps seem also to like the smell of water and streams. Later on in the season, they seem to get bolder and appear in open grassland around their host trees. Host trees are oak, beech, birch and coniferous.

The most obvious feature is the cap, which is brownish in colour and which, in wet weather, sports a slightly sticky, greasy top. It varies in size from 8–18cm across. The camel or fawn-coloured stem or stalk is thick and bulges in an irregular way – sometimes looking like a pot-belly, sometimes like hips overflowing the waistband; sometimes the bulge is close to the cap and resembles a dowager's hump. Under the cap it has pores, rather than gills, which may vary in colour from creamy to yellowish, and sometimes 'olivish' pores that look spongy. The cap is rounded to

hemispherical and flattens slightly on maturity. It can have a pale fawn colour or be a deeper bread-like colour right down to a burnt bread-roll crust appearance. The stems are usually very swollen to look at with something resembling a whitish network towards the top. The flesh is firm, meaty and white throughout the whole cut and the mushroom is as weighty as it looks.

HOW TO PICK

It is a council of perfection to choose a mild, dry day after a rainy period. To prevent squashing and breaking into pieces, it is wise to bring a flat-bottomed basket when hunting for mushrooms. Pick by cutting across the base with a long slim blade or mushroom knife, leaving the mycorrhizal roots attached to the host tree. Pick those that look as fresh as possible. When you bring them home do check the identity of each one.

HOW TO PREPARE

Cut off the earthy base and wipe with a damp clean cloth. Do not peel or you will lose the flavour. They may be eaten cooked and fresh.

TRADITIONAL USES

Ceps thrive in deciduous woodland and it is likely that our ancient ancestors have been gathering and eating them since Neolithic times. Unlike nuts and shellfish, fungi do not normally leave a trace in the archaeological record. However, there is one known find of some mature puffball fungi found preserved in the midden (kitchen rubbish dump) of a Neolithic site in Scotland.

Irish food culture records that if there were more than a few mushrooms for breakfast or supper, we grilled, fried, or baked them, plain or stuffed, or used them in soups, sauces, stews, in tarts and pies, salads, and condiments, and preserved them for winter use in much the same ways as today, except for (perhaps) in oil.

PRESERVING WILD CEPS

• •

Drying is the commonest and easiest method. They may also be preserved in oil, pickled, or made into a ketchup or relish.

POWDERED WILD CEPS

• •

This recipe is adapted from Jane Grigson's book *Mushroom Feast*. In the book she credits it to a pamphlet called *Pottery*, published anonymously. It was, she later discovered, by the London Wine and Food Society; the recipe had been devised in 1946. Just the thing to add flavour and spice during post war rationing! It is a clever way of adding flavour to wild mushrooms - to be dried and powdered and added to soups and stews.

You need sliced wild mushrooms to fill a 2½ litre bowl, together with 1 onion sliced, 5 cloves, 15g powdered mace, and 1 tsp white pepper. Spread the mushrooms and all the other ingredients in a wide pan. Cook very gently until the juices run and then increase the heat until the juices are re-absorbed. Take great care not to let the mushrooms and onion burn. Spread the mushrooms on baking trays and dry in a cool oven (about 90–100°C). When completely dry, crush in a mortar and pestle until you have a fine powder.

Note: You might like to dry them more slowly at a heat below 60°C to prevent any chance of the mushrooms burning. Feel free to experiment with the spices. Use in soups, stews, sauces, tarts, or whatever takes your fancy as a condiment.

WILD CEP AND VENISON BURGER

WHAT GOES IN

- 1kg ground (minced) venison
- 60g dried wild ceps
- 2 large organic onions, peeled and finely chopped
- 120g organic breadcrumbs
- 1 tbsp Worcestershire sauce
- 2 tbsp wild garlic pesto
- 1 organic egg, whisked
- Organic rapeseed oil
- Sea salt and freshly ground organic black pepper

HOW IT GOES

Blitz the dried wild ceps in a processor until ground to a powder. In a large bowl, mix together the minced venison, cep powder, breadcrumbs and onion. Add Worcestershire sauce and wild garlic pesto, fold in the whisked egg and season. Mix until everything is just about combined. Do not overwork the mixture or it will become too dense and the burgers tough. Shape into burger-style patties.

Wild Cep and Venison Burger.

HOW TO FINISH

In a solid cast-iron grill pan over a really high heat using the rapeseed oil or better still grill outside on a 'last of season' barbeques, choosing one of those fab autumn sunset evenings to give your friends a taste of the season.

WHAT YOU GET

I believe that all dried mushrooms have a more pungent dense flavour than their fresh counterparts. Wild ceps really work best with this theory. Combine this with the heady taste of venison and you really have a burger that will turn most heads ... and turn them into a nod of approval!

WILD CEPS ANTI PASTA WITH GARLIC, LEMONS AND OLIVE OIL

For 1kg of wild ceps, take the juice of two lemons, 3–4 cloves garlic, a few bay leaves, peppercorns, 100ml wine vinegar and 60ml rapeseed or olive oil and water, and simmer boil for fifteen minutes. Slice the wild ceps and place in the pot add more water if needed to bring liquid level with the mushrooms. Simmer for five minutes and allow cooling in the liquid. Drain. Place in sterilised jars and cover with oil and a well-fitting cap. Add additional spices or herbs as you wish. Store in a cool, dry place.

WILD CEP SOUP

This happens to be a favourite of one member of the Sugarloaf Convivium. It exists in a copybook of handwritten recipes collected in childhood. Then it was made on a day when a mushroom hunt on a nearby links golf course had yielded more than was needed for breakfast. Later my grown-up hand suggests adding a clove of chopped garlic and small handful of parsley and black pepper.

130g dried wild ceps
4 tablespoons butter
1 thick slice two-day or three-day-old batch loaf
1 litre stock (any stock except that from corned beef or ham)
1 small carton (100ml) cream
About ten twists of a nutmeg grinder
Salt and pepper

Soak the bread in a little of the stock. Wipe and chop the mushrooms into small pieces. Cook them in the butter over a low heat. When the juices run add all the seasonings, the bread and the stock, and stir them around so that the breadcrumbs thicken the soup. In about 10–15 minutes it will be done. Add the cream and allow it to heat through. You may push it through a food mill or even whiz in a processor if you wish. Eat hot or cold.

Native crab apples and smaller Siberian crab apple.

Wild Crab Apple

Malus silvestris * Irish *crann úll fiáin*

> *'An array of truly-fragrant apple-trees, a wood with its pink-tipped bloom.'*
>
> From *'The Vision of MaConglinne'*

In Brehon Law Ireland's native crab apple was listed as one of the seven 'Nobles of the Wood' and known in Old Irish as *crann aball*. There is plenty of evidence that it has been a prized food since man's first arrival in Ireland. There was a distinction between the wild sour apples and the sweeter cultivated type; both were considered valuable. In modern Irish, to distinguish it from cultivated apples, it is called *crann úll fiáin*.

WHERE TO LOOK

Wild crab apples grow in woods, in scrubland, and in road and field hedgerows. It has been a hedgerow plant at least since the eighteenth century so it is common in country lanes.

WHAT IT LOOKS LIKE

A deciduous tree about 6–8m high. The bark is greyish-brown and scaly; the leaves are broad and oval-shaped with serrated edges; the

Native crab apple habitat.

twigs are reddish-brown. In May the flowers appear in clusters of about five, each on a short stalk. They are white with a pinkish tinge. When in fruit, you cannot mistake it as it bears heavy crops of yellow-green fruit, some streaked, or speckled with red. The size of the apple can vary a good deal. It's been suggested that true wild crab apples are small and round and yellow when ripe, and that the trees that bear larger fruits may be descended from cultivated varieties (which were always grafted onto crab-apple root stock) that have reverted to a wild form.

HOW TO PICK

Crap apples can be picked from early September right through to early November. Generally, most are at their best in mid-October. Gather from a place free of traffic fumes. Take several baskets, and a walking-stick to pull down the branches. If they are really ripe, many will already have fallen to the ground. Always gather these first, unless they look too far gone, or have been invaded by wasps or other wildlife that enjoys the fruit. When crabs are ripe sometimes shaking the whole tree, or a single branch, will bring them down. If you plan this method, bring an old blanket and spread it under the tree.

HOW TO PREPARE

All crab apples are scabby and ugly. Do not discard them on that account, as it matters not a whit. Do discard any rotten apples, all the leaves and twigs, and wash with cold water. They are generally cooked without removing skin, core and pips. If not using at once, store in one layer in a cool, dry, airy place.

TRADITIONAL USES

Crab apples are almost always far too sour to be eaten raw. Traditionally they were made into cider, wine, or low-alcohol apple juice and verjuice which was in common use in Europe before malt vinegar was invented. Crab apple jelly is delicious and a delicate pink in colour. Crab apples are high in pectin and enable fruits low in pectin to set to jelly, jam and chutney.

PRESERVING WILD CRAB APPLES

Apples can be preserved, but they also store well just as they are. If you have a cellar or a similar frost-free but cold, dry place, spread them out in plastic or wooden boxes, arranged in one layer so that they do not touch each other. Crab apples are sour thus sugar features in many of the usual methods of preservation. Even cider made from crab apples alone, no matter how dry you like it, is probably going to need some sugar.

Cider and apple wine are traditional. You will need about 12kg of crab apples to give 5 litres of juice. The apples should be left on the trees as long as possible but not exposed to hard frosts. Then they should be shaped into a heap and allowed to mature for a few weeks in a shady frost-free place, before crushing or pressing.

Preserving wild crab apples as a verjuice is really a very slightly fermented sharp cider-like liquid used in place of vinegar or lemon juice. The apples should be left on the trees as long as possible but gathered before the first frost. Take a bucketful of crab apples and find a reasonably clean, shady place to pile them in a heap. After 3–4 days, once they begin to sweat, sort them out, discarding stalks and any decayed, or rotten fruit. Return to your bucket. Next extract the juice. Strain through a jelly bag. Place in a bottle and store in a cool place for at least four weeks before using it. Use in place of lemon juice in recipes. Think of verjuice as a gentle acidulant. It tastes tart, a bit like lemon juice or vinegar but not as harsh, great on salads or use as an alternative in recipes.

WILD CRAB APPLE
AND ROSE HIP JELLY

WHAT GOES IN

1½kg wild crab apples

½kg wild rose hips, prepared

Cinnamon or spices, to taste, if
you wish

1kg sugar

Water, just enough to get the juices running

HOW IT GOES

Simmer rosehips in a pot for 2 hours, press through a sieve. Chop the apples, bring to the boil and simmer separately until soft. Combine the rosehip pulp, crab apples and juice and strain liquid overnight through muslin, without forcing by squeezing.

HOW TO FINISH

First, take clear liquid and measure it, adding 1kg sugar to every litre of juice. Place in a pot with sugar, stir and when sugar is dissolved boil rapidly until setting point 106° is reached. Skim and pour into sterilised jars. Cover and store in a cool dry place.

Second, twist the muslin and force the pulpy mixture through, pour into sterilised jars, cover, and store in a cool dry place.

Third, take the pulp, press through a sieve to remove cores and seeds. Spread this on a dehydrator tray or baking tray. Dehydrate or place on baking trays in as low an oven as possible, overnight or until dry.

Wild Crab Apple and Rose Hip Jelly.

WHAT YOU GET

One set of ingredients, three results and no waste!

A clear wild rosehip and wild crab apple jelly: That works beautifully and simply toasted with a goat's cheese, or as an old-fashioned 'fruit butter or cheese' as accompaniment to a vintage cheese. Also works a treat with pork, turkey or chicken and makes a great accompaniment to a traditional meatloaf or as the sweet ingredient if you're making your own muffins.

Also a cloudy wild rosehip and wild crab apple cordial: Perfect as a chilled cordial with water for the kids instead of the mainstream stuff, just add sugar syrup to sweeten. Also perfect for the adults as 'a teaspoon of autumn' with a glass of bubbly. Chill well after opening or, if needed, freeze.

Finally, a dried wild rosehip and wild crab apple pulp: Cut into cubes or thin slices, you can use it with your granola or muesli in the morning; or added to your favourite bread or scone recipes.

WILD CRAB APPLE PECTIN STOCK

Many fruits and berries are low in pectin. Having a few litres of this in the store cupboard is sensible and enables sweet preserves to be easily made.

2kg wild crab apples
1¼ litre water

Cut the crab apples in halves. Put in a pot with the water and simmer gently for about 45 minutes or until pulped. Strain through a jelly bag and pour the resulting stock through a funnel into sterilised jars or bottles. Seal. Store in a cool, dry, dark place. 300ml of the stock will set 4kg of any fruit that is low in pectin.

WILD CRAB APPLE AND WILD MINT 'BUTTER'

  1kg wild crab apples
  1kg sugar, warmed
  800ml water
  Juice of one lemon
  A huge handful of wild mint, destalked and chopped

Cut crab apples in half and stew in the water until soft. Strain. Put in a pot with the lemon juice and sugar. Stir until sugar is dissolved. Bring to the boil and continue stirring. This mixture splutters, so wear long sleeves and gloves. Continue until the mixture thickens. You can test if it is thick enough by spooning a little on a cold plate and allowing it to cool. If a skin forms, it has reached the correct consistency for a fruit butter. Take off the heat and stir in the chopped mint. Taste, adding more mint if you wish. Pour into sterilised jars and cover. Store in a cool dry place.

Note: You may, if you wish, cook until the mixture is thick enough to be a cheese. Follow the instructions for fruit cheese in the Preservation section. If you plan to serve this as a condiment with lamb or mutton, a cheese is a better choice.

Note: A similar butter can be made using different herbs such as sage, marjoram or thyme.

Wild Elderberry

Sambucus nigra * Irish *caorthroim*

The wild elder (*see also* elderflower) is one of a number of indigenous shrub-like trees that became common about six thousand years ago following forest clearance by the first farmers on the island. In ancient Ireland trees were accorded magic qualities and were symbols of the agricultural year. White blossom was a sign of spring and the purplish black berries a sign of fulfillment of the harvest and renewed life.

WHERE TO LOOK

Elder is a common tree all over Europe. In Ireland you'll find it in hedgerows, beside footpaths, in neglected and recently cleared woodland, in parks and gardens.

WHAT IT LOOKS LIKE

Elder is an untidy, many-stemmed, shrub tree, rarely more than 5 metres high; the bark is corky and grey-white in colour. It has 5-7 elliptical, finely-toothed, soft, green leaves. In late summer the flowerheads turn into reddish clusters of small berries which as they ripen turn purple/black and, depending on aspect and altitude, are normally ready for picking in September. A good sign

that the berries are ripe enough is that the bracts carrying the clusters of berries turn upside down and hang down.

HOW TO PICK

Bring with you a large basket or plastic bucket and a walking-stick with a curved handle; a crutch also works well, so does a shepherd's crook. Anything that will draw the branches close enough to cut the berry cluster off, or nip it off with your nails. Choose a place well away from traffic fumes and busy roads; look for trees with plenty of very dark red/purple-black fully-ripe berries and avoid those that have begun to wrinkle.

HOW TO PREPARE

Give them a quick shake to discard stray leaves and the odd insect.

Many experts advise a quick rinse with water. However, if the berries are intended for wine, washing removes the natural yeasts. Strip the berries from the stalks with a fork. Wear gloves as the juice does stain the skin.

TRADITIONAL USES

Traditionally wild elderberries were eaten fresh, or preserved by drying, preserved with vinegar, with sugar, made into wine or chutney, into bottled sauces, used to flavour vinegar and a variety of drinks and syrups as well as desserts, cakes and biscuits. In a good year they make good wine or can be used to flavour spirits. They were made into cordials and syrups, jams and jellies (often with crab apples or other hedgerow berries). There are many references to 'pontack sauce' a spicy sauce made with vinegar or red wine and often used to add flavour to organ meats like liver, kidneys and hearts.

PRESERVING ELDERBERRIES

Whole berries in sugar syrup are delicious and versatile. They make a wonderful flavouring for spirits and, with crab apples for pectin, a deep rich-coloured jelly and a fruit syrup. With two kilos of berries and a couple of kilos of sugar you can transform them into five litres of deep rich wine with a flavour reminiscent of port. Methods for ultilising the berries in any of these ways may be found in the Preservation section.

Wild Elderberry and Orange Pudding.
• •

WILD ELDERBERRY AND
ORANGE PUDDING

WHAT GOES IN

30g organic wholewheat flour

150g organic brown breadcrumbs

150g elderberries

120g organic sugar

120g organic butter (unsalted)

350g organic marmalade

1 organic orange zest

3 organic eggs

1 tsp bicarbonate of soda (bread soda)

1 tsp boiling water

HOW IT GOES

In a bowl, mix the wholewheat flour, brown breadcrumbs and sugar together. Melt the butter with the marmalade in a saucepan. Then add the orange zest and elderberries. Whisk the eggs until fluffy and gently fold into the mixture. Dissolve soda with boiling water and whisk into mixture.

HOW TO FINISH

Pour into a pudding bowl, and do as your grandmother did. Place parchment paper over the top and seal with a lid or with tinfoil and twine and steam in a deep pot of boiling water for 2 hours. Alternatively, if you want to be more fancy and modern, you can pour into individual ramekins or cups and cook similarly.

WHAT YOU GET

Is a pudding, lighter than a winter one, but still with enough weight to signify that autumn is here and that we seem to need something more unctuous. (This is the Strawberry Tree version of Shirley Spears' original 'Three Chimneys' Hot Marmalade Pudding recipe from The Isle of Skye.)

WILD ELDERBERRY SYRUP

3kg wild elderberries
¾ litre water

Place the berries and water in a large pot. Bring to boiling point and simmer for 45 minutes. Strain it through a jelly bag, leaving it to drip overnight. Next day measure the juice and add the required amount of sugar. The juice is measured and sugar calculated at the rate of 300g per litre. It was traditional to tie a few cloves in a jelly muslin bag. You may like to experiment with other spices. Warm the sugar. Meanwhile, bring the juice back to the boil and simmer for a few minutes. Add sugar, stir until dissolved, and boil for about 15 minutes, or until the juice is of a light syrup consistency. Skim to ensure the syrup is clear. Bottle in small sterilised bottles with tightly-fitting caps. Small bottles are best because the syrup needs to be used within a reasonable time once opened. If you require really long storage, follow the method for bottling in the Preservation section.

PONTACK SAUCE

500ml vinegar or claret, boiling hot

500ml wild elderberries

1 onion, very finely chopped

40 peppercorns

14 cloves

1 blade mace

1 tsp salt

½ tsp ground ginger

This sauce is what Mrs Beaton describes as a store sauce – what now is called a condiment, like Yorkshire relish. There are numerous references to it in old cookbooks and even descriptions of meals, but finding out exactly how it was made proved elusive. It is spicy and sharp if made with vinegar, rather less so if made with 'claret' as an old recipe suggests.

Take a deep ovenproof dish and pour the boiling vinegar or wine over the berries. Cover and place in a very, very low oven (below 50°C) overnight. Strain the liquid and put it in a pot with all the other ingredients. Cook at boiling point for 10 minutes. Pour the liquid with the spices into small sterilised bottles with tightly-fitting caps. Traditionally used to enhance liver and other organ meats.

WILD ELDERBERRY CHUTNEY

1kg wild elderberries

1 large onion, finely chopped

75g raisins

1kg crab apples, washed and chopped roughly

½ litre wine or cider vinegar

75-100g brown sugar (or to taste)

1 tsp salt

¼ tsp freshly ground black pepper

Spices, as desired. The amount and variety is a personal choice: consider nutmeg, cinnamon, mace, cloves, allspice, ginger, mustard seed, and chilli. Don't go mad with too many, or add too much. The balance of the sweet/sour flavour is also a matter of taste – some people like rather sweet chutney, some prefer a sour one. Add less sugar to start and see how you go – it's easy to add more.

Put the elderberries in a preserving pot and give them a good mash. Add the rest of the ingredients. Bring to the boil and simmer for about 12–16 minutes, or until thick. Do your final tasting at this time and make any adjustments you wish. Stir well for another minute over heat. Pour through a wide-necked funnel into sterilised jars. It is better if the covers are not metal. Store in a cool dark place and allow to mature for several months.

Wild Hazelnut

Corylus avellana * Irish *cnó coill*

Hazels were gathered and eaten by the earliest settlers who arrived in Ireland in Mesolithic times over nine thousand years ago. Along with Scots pine, hazel was the dominant tree for a thousand years and remains to this day a significant species in woodland within limestone regions. The extensive wildwoods of ash and hazel in the Burren in County Clare show how it recolonises abandoned land as long as the soil is alkaline. However, it will grow pretty well any-where, as long as conditions are reasonably dry and well drained.

A useful trick to make a wild hazel tree produce more nuts is to use a technique called 'brutt'. In late summer visit the tree. On each branch of the current season's growth will be a shoot about 30cm long. Break this shoot about halfway along its length and leave it to hang down. This opens up the bush and encourages more female flowers to form. Then when winter comes visit the hazel tree again and snip off the brutted shoot to about 3–4 buds.

In Irish tradition hazel is the Tree of Knowledge and one of the 'Nobles' of the wood in the tree lists. Apart from many uses for its wood (from divining for water to warding off evil) hazelnuts were a vital source of protein and were easy to preserve for the winter. Correctly done, hazelnuts can keep for a year and must have been a valuable winter food. It is clear that there was a trade in hazelnuts.

The Annals of Ulster record that in the year 1097 the nuts (*cnó coill*) were so abundant that a *seisedach* could be bought for a penny. This year was known as the year of the white nuts. *Seisedach* used to mean a sixth of dry goods and may refer to a sixth of a sack, although what size the sack was, or how much a penny was worth, is difficult to know.

WHERE TO LOOK

The Burren in the west of Ireland is famous for its expanse of wildwood hazel scrub. Hazel is common, especially in alkaline limestone areas. The soil does not need to be rich or sheltered and the trees will grow at high altitudes. They often grow as an understorey shrub in mixed woodlands of beech, oak, and ash. You'll also find them in hedgerows, on abandoned ground, and in scrub.

WHAT IT LOOKS LIKE

Somewhere between a shrub and a tree, they can grow up to 5

metres. The bark is a silver- or coppery-brown and the twigs a reddish-brown. The leaves grow alternately on the twig and up to 12cm long. They are broad in shape with a point at the top and a heart shape at the base. The flowers appear before the leaves; the male in the form of a catkin and the female enclosed within a bud less than a ½cm in size. The fruits, which can grow as a solitary nut or in clusters, are encased in an ethereal green husk that loses colour as it ripens. The nut within is between round and egg-shaped, starting pale and ripening to brown with a woody shell.

HOW TO PICK

Hazelnuts hide behind the leaves to the point that a tree may look as if it bears no crop. Hazelnuts are best gathered when they are mature almost to the point when they are ready to fall, normally in mid-autumn. Choose a dry day and gather in a sack or basket.

HOW TO PREPARE

Damp nuts will go mouldy. When you get home remove the husks and discard any nuts showing signs of mould and those with grey or dark shells. Store in a sack or basket in a cool dry place until you are ready to use.

TRADITIONAL USES

There was an ancient tradition of preserving hazelnuts in mead (a drink made from honey). They were dried, preserved in salt and fried in butter, plain and spiced, and widely used in the baking of cakes, biscuits and puddings, and in a savoury stuffing. Many were simply eaten as a protein-rich winter food. In Yorkshire they were mixed with honey to produce a sweet. In north-western Italy they were made into a condiment (or store cupboard sauce) containing olive oil, parsley, garlic and onions and used to enrich soup and pasta sauces.

PRESERVING HAZELNUTS

The simplest and most traditional method is to remove the outer green husk and allow to dry off for a few days, followed by storage in cool conditions. An equally good way is to prepare as for drying and then place in alternate layers of clean, dry sand, finishing with sand. Store in a dry place.

Fully-peeled nuts with the inner skin removed can be made into a variety of nut butters and, with oil, into sauces similar to Italian *pesto* and French *pistou* and Irish wild garlic pesto.

WILD HAZELNUT CHOCOLATE CHIP BISCUITS

WHAT GOES IN

100g wild hazelnuts, shelled
185g organic sugar
115g organic butter

WILD HAZELNUT

1 organic egg

165g organic flour

175g organic 70% dark chocolate, chopped to crumb

A scant tsp sea salt

HOW IT GOES

Roast hazelnuts in the oven for 8–10 minutes at 170°C. Remove and place in a damp clean tea towel and rub hazelnuts together to remove skins and then finely chop the de-skinned hazelnuts.

Cream the butter and sugar together, add the egg and continue mixing. Add in the sieved flour, salt, and mix until well combined. Fold in the wild hazelnuts and crumbed chocolate. Place mixture in cling film and leave in fridge for 10 minutes.

HOW TO FINISH

Divide mixture into 30g portions and roll into balls and flatten on to parchment paper on an oven tray, with space to spread. Bake at 150°C for 15 minutes approx. Remove, and cool. Yields about 28 biscuits.

WHAT YOU GET

Is a taste of autumn with the wild hazelnuts and, besides, it makes for a really good excuse to have a chocolate chip biscuit.

WILD RABBIT BRAISED WITH WILD HAZELNUTS AND WILD THYME

1kg wild rabbit, jointed

2 tbsp wild blackberry vinegar, or sherry, optional

2 tbsp olive or rapeseed oil

110ml dry white wine or dry sherry

110ml chicken or rabbit stock

2 tbsp wild thyme leaves

4 cloves

A pinch of freshly ground nutmeg

Sea salt and freshly ground black pepper

90g wild hazelnuts, shelled and inner skin removed

8 fresh wild garlic leaves or oil preserved ones

1 slice good quality bread

Sprinkle the vinegar over the rabbit pieces and allow to marinate overnight. If the rabbit is young and tender, you can skip this bit.

Heat the oil in a large pan, season the rabbit pieces and brown in the pan over a gentle heat on all sides. Remove from the pan, and place in a wide shallow, oven-proof casserole.

Deglaze the pan with the stock, add wine or sherry and bubble up. Add the wild thyme. Place in the oven set at 150°C to continue cooking for about 20 minutes or until the rabbit pieces are tender and done through.

Meanwhile, toast the hazelnuts. Fry the bread slice over a high heat, in a little olive or rapeseed oil. Blitz the bread, nuts, wild garlic, cloves and nutmeg in a processor until you have a purée. This is used to add flavour and thicken the liquid in the casserole. Stir in until it is well mixed, check seasoning and serve hot.

Native wild rose hip.

Wild Rose

* *

Rosa canina *Irish *conrós**

The native wild rose of these islands *Rosa canina* (usually called the common rose, dog rose, briar rose, hip tree or itchy backs) is a bush with thorns and small, loose-petalled white and palest pink blooms in summer. The other almost equally widespread species is the naturalised *Rosa rugosa* (the Japanese rose). *Rosa rugosa*, tolerates salt spray and wind and increases rapidly by means of suckers. It is found as a hedgerow plant in coastal areas and, more recently, planted on road embankments. The hips of both types are edible and can be used to make jellies, preserves, sauces and wine.

Rose hips have been eaten since ancient times and in the Irish tree lists it is relegated to a fourth-class tree alongside brambles and bog myrtles. In mediaeval times wild roses were grown in monasteries as a medicinal herb. It had the great virtue of being high in a number of nutrients, especially vitamin C. Rose hip syrup contains 300mg per 100g weight. This is up to four times more than blackcurrant juice and twenty times as much as the juice of an orange. That is the reason why it was part of the war effort to gather rose hips and turn them into syrup for use as a vitamin drink to prevent scurvy in the population, especially in children, during the Second World War.

WHERE TO LOOK

Hedgerows, waste land, at the edges of woodlands, abandoned homesteads, often growing alongside brambles. *Rosa rugosa* is common near the seashore, spreading in the hedgerows from houses, and along road and railway embankments.

WHAT IT LOOKS LIKE

The native wild rose is an upright but straggly shrub and can grow up to 3 metres high, often piggy-backing on other hedge-row shrubs and trees for support. It comes into leaf in spring. The leaves have a single leader and the rest grow opposite each other in either 4 or 6 pairs. They are sharply-toothed at the edges and soft to the touch. The flowers, which are white or pale pink, bloom any time between late April and July. In early autumn you see the hips forming. They are like a narrow-topped urn in shape, orange at first then turning towards red. Wait to gather them un-til October and after the first frosts which soften them. The hips do stay on the bush for far longer but it is generally advised to pick them before the end of October. Scientific evidence for this advice cannot be found. It may simply be the folk tradition that, after that date, the *púca* breathes, or spits (or worse) on all berries!

The Japanese rose is far shorter and tougher in texture, has more abundant leaves (arranged without a leader and in about 4-6 pairs). The flowers are larger and are a striking deep pink-ish-purple. The hips are much larger and squat, like a flattened sphere in shape, with a little tuft at the base of the flower on the top. They are a repeat flowering rose so you might be tempted to gather them during the summer. Although it is not traditional, a short period of artificial frost will soften them effectively.

HOW TO PICK

A berry picker really comes into its own. Not only are there thorns on the bush but remember the nickname itchy? Rose hips and seeds are covered with fine hairs that can irritate the skin and cause severe internal damage. So do not let children eat them raw or shove them inside clothes. Wear gloves and long sleeves. The best berries are at the top of the bush so bring a walking-stick or crook. Pulling down a branch gently and pushing the berry picker upwards from the tip is the most efficient way. Pick plenty; a kilo of hips will yield about 1¼ litres of syrup.

Native wild rose blooms.

HOW TO PREPARE

Remove any stalks and rinse with cold water and drain well. When ready to cook, have everything prepared as, when crushed, they must be cooked at once to avoid vitamin loss.

TRADITIONAL USES

Making them into a syrup is the most common use, followed by rose hip wine (which was sometimes made with rose hips preserved in syrup), rosehip and crab apple jam or jelly, and as one ingredient in a mixed hedgerow jam or jelly. Traditional in Northern Europe, especially in Hungary, Germany and the Scandinavian countries, are fruit soups which, in winter, are often made from diluted fruit syrups, including rose hip syrup. A preserve made of a purée of rose hips can be used for tarts and other desserts and puddings.

PRESERVING ROSE HIPS

Note: No matter what recipe you use it is important that you strain cooked hips through a fine mesh strainer in order to remove the hairs and seeds that cause irritation.

Drying

AIR DRYING: Wash the hips and spread out on rack to dry in a sunny, airy spot indoors. They will take up to two weeks at room temperature.

DRYING IN A DEHYDRATOR will take five or six hours.

OVEN DRYING: Spread washed hips on roasting trays. Dry for one hour at 50°C and leave in oven to cool. Repeat this seven days in a row.

Storing dried rose hips. These are best stored in a cardboard or wooden box in a cool, dry, dark place.

Preserving with sugar for jams, jelly, pastes and syrup & preserving with sugar and yeast to make wine

Follow individual recipe instructions, but again if using fresh rose hips (rather than rose hip syrup), ensure that all seeds and hairs are strained out.

Preserving as a bottled tea (short-term storage)

Crush, mince using a coarse setting, or process very briefly in a food processor.

WILD ROSE HIP SYRUP

WHAT GOES IN
700g wild rosehips
600g organic sugar
2 litres water
Juice of an organic lemon

HOW IT GOES

Remove the stalks, wash and chop the rosehips and place in saucepan with 1 litre of water. Bring to the boil and simmer for 20 minutes until soft. Strain through a fine-mesh sieve, and return to the saucepan, adding about the same amount of water as before and simmer again for 20 minutes. Strain again, and simmer for another 20 minutes. Finally, strain all the liquid through a 'muslin cloth' into a clean saucepan. Add in the sugar and lemon juice. Bring slowly to the boil and simmer for 30 minutes until syrupy. Remove and skim off any froth.

HOW TO FINISH

Pour into sterilised Kilner jars and seal. Sugar density is the preservative here. Our grandmothers would have said this would keep for a whole year or more in a cool pantry … it seems to have worked, because we, the grandchildren are alive to read this, so you decide!

WHAT YOU GET

Rose hips pack more vitamin C than our new-found beloved orange. Here is a fab syrup brimming with summer sunshine. Use it diluted with water as a refreshing drink. Mix through a natural organic yoghurt. It's perfect at breakfast time, either served on a pancake or as a topping for your porridge.

WILD ROSE HIP SOUP

This is probably more suitable for consuming as a cold fruit soup.

    ¾kg fresh rose hips (about 350g dried)
    1¾ litre water
    1 stick cinnamon
    3 tbsp lemon juice
    1 strip lemon peel
    A large glass of white wine
    Sugar to taste
    A little arrowroot

Simmer the rose hips in the water until soft. Put through a fine sieve to remove seeds and hairs. Put back into the hot water with the cinnamon, lemon juice and peel, and all but a tablespoon or so of the wine. Add a few tablespoons of sugar and simmer for about five minutes. Taste for sweetness adding as much sugar as desired and stir until dissolved. Dissolve the arrowroot in the remaining wine and stir into the soup. Bring back to simmering point, stirring all the time. If serving hot, serve at once with a little whipped cream, or crème fraiche, or sour cream. If serving cold, chill for a couple of hours before serving as above.

WILD ROSE HIP PURÉE

Dating from the mediaeval period, this is probably one of the oldest recipes for preserving rose hips for festive tarts during the winter months. No doubt honey rather than sugar was used. It is a tad labour intensive and best to use thin surgical-style gloves to prevent skin irritation.

½kg rose hips
Sugar or honey (equal to the weight of the prepared flesh)

Cut open the wild rose hips and remove all the seeds, hairs and pith. Place in a wide-necked glass or earthenware jar for several days until they soften. You will hasten this by giving them a stir every so often. Put them through a very fine-mesh sieve. Using an equal weight of the resulting purée and sugar, warm gently, just enough to dissolve the sugar. Pour into a sterilised jar and sterilise as described in the recipe for wild rose hip syrup.

WILD ROSE HIP TART

1 jar of preserved wild rose hip purée (see recipe above)
1 fully baked, shallow rich shortcrust pastry case
3–4 tbsp rose hip jelly
Crystalised rose petals (optional)

Spread the rose hip purée over the bottom of the pastry. Melt the jelly and pour over the purée. Allow to set before serving. Decorate with crystallised rose petals.

Wild Sloe

• • • • • • • • • • • • • • • • • • • •

Prunus spinosa * Irish *áirne an draighean dubh*

Sloes are the fruit of the blackthorn tree. The Irish word *áirne* means sour. So sour that it is hard to believe that it is related to all the luscious plums of the garden, or all of the sweet plums and fruits of the plum family. Despite its sour taste, it has been eaten since ancient times. In mediaeval monasteries it was turned into an alcoholic drink. The folk practice continued with sloe-flavoured distilled *poitín* and, more legally, by adding sloes to flavour gin.

WHERE TO LOOK

The wild sloe grows in hedgerows pretty well everywhere there are fields to enclose, although they are not so prolific where field boundaries are made of stone. With its sharp spikes it makes the perfect stock-proof hedging plant and with spreading suckers it spreads quickly into an impenetrable barrier.

WHAT IT LOOKS LIKE

A dense tree-like shrub that can grow up to 3 metres high. What distinguishes this shrub are the long spiky thorns. In winter the blackish-brown bark is bare and dark in colour; then early in spring

prolific white flowers grow along the full length of the branch. Then dark-green, oval-shaped leaves develop and fruits form that turn from green to purple to almost black with a bloom of natural yeast on the skin.

You must wait until after the first hard frosts before gathering them. The skins are thick and the frost makes them more porous and easier to process. The leaves have usually fallen before this occurs, making them easy to spot in the hedgerows. Sloes, like plums and damsons, flower and fruit best when the temperature the winter before has fallen below minus 7°C for at least a week or ten days.

HOW TO PICK

Choose a place away from traffic fumes and wear a long-sleeved thorn-proof jacket and tightly fitting gloves (old leather ones are ideal). A strong berry picker is useful, but be careful of the thorns.

HOW TO PREPARE

Spread out on a flat surface and remove the berries from the twigs and leaves. If you have a garden sieve to hand, it is a useful way of doing this. As for washing, if you do so there is a danger of washing off the natural yeast, which shows as a bloom on the skin.

TRADITIONAL USES

No one in their right mind would eat a sloe from the tree. They are intensely astringent, sour and bitter. How clever our ancestors must have been to devise ways of making them palatable. Like olives they have to be treated either with frost, heat, cooking with sugar or honey, soaking in alcohol, brewed into wine, or distilled. Indeed, there are references in the literature to a monastic tradition of doing just that, distilling into spirits. The English tradition of flavouring gin with sloes and sugar results in well-flavoured, claret-coloured liqueur.

Fresh sloes may be preserved in sugar syrup, or with sugar to make jelly or jam, in wine and in spirits.

Being a stoned fruit, sloes take longer to dry than berries – up to 4 weeks at room temperature. Spread washed sloes out on rack to dry in a sunny, airy spot indoors. Drying in a dehydrator will take 6–8 hours. To oven dry, spread washed sloes on roasting trays. Dry for 1 hour in a cooling oven at 50°C and leave in oven to cool. Repeat this for 7 days in a row. Once dry they are as resilient as raisins and seem to last forever, store in a Kilner jar in a cool, dry, dark place.

WILD SLOE GIN
MACAROONS

WHAT GOES IN

Macaroon mix:

3 organic egg whites

10g caster or organic fine sugar

10g muscovado sugar

140g icing sugar

90g ground organic almonds

Sloe gin filling:

100g organic creamed cheese

50g organic butter

100g icing sugar

1 tbsp wild sloe gin pulp (*see* sloe gin recipe)

HOW IT GOES

Sieve icing sugar and ground almonds together. Whisk the egg whites in a bowl until soft peaks form. Add caster sugar, combine; then, add muscovado sugar. Whisk until you have stiff peaks.

Add to icing sugar and ground almonds, folding quickly to create your batter/mix.

Place the mix in piping bag and pipe macaroons onto a tray lined with grease-proof paper. Bake at 150°C for 10–12 minutes. Remove and cool.

HOW TO FINISH

For the filling, Whisk the cream cheese and butter together until combined smoothly; then, add icing sugar and combine again. Fold sloe gin pulp into mix. Fill into piping bag and pipe mix onto the flat side of one macaroon then sandwich together with the second one.

WHAT YOU GET

Is a 'French style' macaroon and a great way to use that fab sloe-ginny pulp that you have strained from your sloe gin. Perfect as a Christmas present for your friends … well those who are not already receiving a wild sloe gin gift

Wild Sloe Gin Macaroons.

SLOE GIN

The amount of sugar you use determines whether this results in wild sloe schnapps or a wild sloe liqueur. This version is our favourite and when complete should be served straight from the freezer, ice cold in shot glasses, to share with your friends at Christmas.

1 bottle really good gin divided (it's for your friends, only the best!)

Enough sugar to fill one third of the bottle

Enough wild sloes to fill one half of the bottle

A few shelled and peeled almonds (optional)

Fill the bottle one third full of sugar. Each sloe must be pierced with a sharp fork or a darning needle and placed at once into the bottle (therapy!). Top up with the spirit of your choice and refit the cap tightly. Shake to help dissolve the sugar and release the juice of the sloes. Shake once a day for seven days and once a week for seven weeks. Halfway through, you can add the almonds. At first the liquid will be tinged with pink and over the weeks it will darken into a rich purple.

Christmas is the traditional time to open the bottle. In reality, it is better if left for several more months. Strain and decant the liquid alone into a fresh bottle.

Now shake out the wild sloes, and this is the best part. Pass through a mill and use the boozy pulp to add flavour to a dessert. Syllabub, fruit fools, ice cream, tipsy cake, boozy fairy cakes, cheesecake, plumb and almond tart immediately spring to mind, but it is also tasty in scones, brioche, breads, or even winter puds.

WILD SLOE BERRY CORDIAL

Sloes develop natural yeast, which shows as a bloom on the skin, this needs to be fully washed off for this drink.

Enough wild sloes to half a fill half a bottle
Enough sugar to almost half fill a bottle
Boiled water, cooled to lukewarm

Add sugar to bottle. Prick the sloes with a fork or darning needle and place in bottle. Top up with the water. Cap really firmly and shake. Store at room temperature. Shake once a day for seven days and once a week for seven weeks. Strain and decant the liquid alone into a fresh bottle. Drink diluted. Now shake out the wild sloes, and this is the best part as in the sloe gin recipe above; the sloes might not be boozy, but they definitely have been sweetened and can be used in all the recipe ideas for sloe berry pulp.

Gifts from the Wild Food Kitchen

• • • • • • • • • • • • • • • • • •

Everyone loves to receive a handmade gift. A pot of homemade jam or a box of homemade sweets or biscuits is worth a thousand boxes of chocolates or fancy biscuits. Homemade food is the surest way of showing how much you value a relationship, appreciate their friendship, or return their love.

Combine a wild food you have picked, prepared, preserved in a pretty jar or box and the effect is even stronger. You are giving them something they cannot buy, a taste they may never have encountered.

There are scores of recipes and hundreds of suggestion of how to turn wild food into a wide variety of items that are suitable for making and giving as gifts from your wild food kitchen.

You can, of course, buy jars, bottles and boxes or simply collect them, soak off labels and disguise any printing on the caps or the outside of boxes with pretty summery material or paper, and attach your own design for your Wild Food Kitchen label. Alternatively, pack into small serving dishes that form part of the gift.

Light baskets are inexpensive to buy and are an attractive way of presenting a number of wild food gifts:

- Fruit and berry liqueurs such as wild sloe gin, wild strawberry schnapps, wild hawthorn blossom liqueur and wild hawthorn berry brandy.

- Country wines and beers like wild elderflower champagne, wild rose hip wine and nettle beer.

- Unusual and delicious soft drinks and cordials like wild elderflower lemonade, wild elderflower or wild blackberry cordial, elderberry cordial, wild rose hip cordial.

- Store cupboard sauces and condiments like wild elderberry pontack sauce, wild mushroom ketchup or dried, powdered wild mushrooms, wild blackberry vinegar, wild sorrel 'green' sauce, wild crab apple and wild mint sauce.

- Luxurious bottled wild fruits such as wild strawberry, wild damson, wild bilberry, wild elderberry.

- Aromatic and richly-flavoured syrups and dessert

sauces made from wild elderflower, wild elderberry, wild bilberry, wild blackberry or wild strawberry.

* Jam, jelly, fruit butter to spread on scones, or cakes or use in desserts. Fruit cheeses to eat with cheese, game and cooked meat and poultry like rowanberry, bilberry, elderberry, crab apple, hawthorn berry, wild damson, wild blackberry and wild crap apple.

* Rich, tangy chutney made from wild elderberry, wild crab apple, wild blackberry.

* Homemade savoury biscuits like wild dillisk oatcakes; sweet biscuits and cakes flavoured with wild berries and wild hazelnuts.

* Spiced wild hazelnuts.

* Pickles made from wild rock samphire, wild field mushrooms, wild ceps, wild St George's mushrooms.

* Delicious oil-preserved wild foods like wild garlic, and wild garlic pesto and wild mushroom antipasta or wild sorrel.

* Bunches of dried wild herbs and blossoms like wild mint, wild thyme, dillisk, carrageen, wild elderflower, meadowsweet, and jars of dried wild mushrooms.

* Delicate crystallised wild flowers such as wild primrose, wild violet, wild rose petals.

Index